LUTHER'S THEOLOGICAL
DEVELOPMENT FROM
ERFURT TO AUGSBURG

AMS PRESS
NEW YORK

LANDMARKS IN HISTORY

Edited by BERNADOTTE E. SCHMITT

LUTHER'S THEOLOGICAL DEVELOPMENT FROM ERFURT TO AUGSBURG

BY

ALBERT HYMA

University of Michigan

NEW YORK

F. S. CROFTS & CO.

1928

Reprinted from the edition of 1928, New York
First AMS EDITION published 1971
Manufactured in the United States of America

International Standard Book Number: 0-404-03479-9

Library of Congress Number: 76-137247

AMS PRESS INC.
NEW YORK, N.Y. 10003

CONTENTS

CONTENTS

HISTORICAL INTRODUCTION

Martin Luther is one of those few dynamic figures in world history whose career will long remain of enduring interest to many thousands of serious-minded students. What the Reformation would have been without his leadership is difficult to conceive, but it is certain that his personality was the dominating factor in its early development. The whole movement, in fact, bears the ineffaceable impress of his struggle with late medieval traditions. Luther had his precursors. He was in part the product of his environment; he was a German of the Germans, and his mind bore the imprints of a multitude of forces. But far from being the passive recipient of opinions new and old, he chose to blaze the way for millions of faithful followers. He became for half of Europe the man of destiny, whose activities personified the greatest issues of the time.

The Reformation as a religious movement, without the dynamic personality of Martin Luther, is little more than an empty shell. Hence the importance of the greatest problem in Luther's life,—the development of his theology from 1505 to 1530. In recent years a flood of light has been thrown upon Luther's experiences in Erfurt and Wittenberg. Not only have the discoveries of new sources revealed a wealth of new material, but a group of scholars, both Protestant and Roman Catholic, have sought to interpret the sources, giving to the public, in a huge mass of books and articles, the result of their painstaking investigations. Although the authorities do not agree on the relative value of the various sources, nor on the solution of the problems connected with Luther's early life, they have at least enabled us to gain a clear view of the whole situation.

Luther's ancestors were mostly Thuringian farmers, who transmitted to their illustrious descendant much that distinguished him in manner and temperament from his associates in university and monastery. His father, Hans Luther, had moved from Thuringia to Eisleben in the county of Mansfeld near Saxony. It was here, on November 10, 1483, that Martin was born. Half a year later the parents tried to improve their living by settling in the city of Mansfeld, a flourishing center of iron industry. For several years they remained very poor, but by the year 1491 they had risen above the rank and file of the poorer classes. One should, therefore, be cautious not to lay too much stress on these early years of poverty, inasmuch as Martin cannot have remembered much that transpired before he had reached the age of eight.

More significant, however, was the character of the parents. They were of the opinion that children should always render implicit obedience to their elders, and that severe physical punishments were often beneficial. "My mother once flogged me," wrote Martin later, "on account of a nut, till the blood flowed." He later deplored the treatment he had received from his parents, but at the same time he cherished a lasting affection towards them, for he realized perfectly that his lot had been simply like that of most children of his time. Furthermore, he recalled that there used to be many joyous moments when both father and mother were kind and cheerful.

There is no justification in the assumption that Martin Luther's revolt against the Church can be traced to his father's attitude toward this institution. Hans Luther was a loyal church member, in whose home the children learned the Lord's Prayer, the Apostles' Creed, and the Ten Commandments. He does not seem to have had the means to secure a German Bible, for Martin relates that only at a later period he became acquainted with the Bible. However, legends about his discovery of a copy in the University Library, covered with dust, are not based on facts. For when he was still a boy, probably at Magdeburg, he had read several parts of the Old and New Testaments.

Martin Luther was as loyal to the Church as his father had been before him. Not only did he devoutly accept the teachings of the clergy, but he would gladly have helped to burn heretics. It was not until he had himself been denounced as a heretic that he began to sympathize with them. That the thought of the Last Judgment always filled him with terror was no more surprising than that he had a very realistic conception of the devil, witches, and other evil spirits. His own mother, he tells, ascribed the death of one of his brothers to the machinations of a neighbor, whom she considered a witch. Luther merely conformed to the superstitions of his age. His youthful mind was plastic enough to receive both the good and the bad notions of his contemporaries. It proved to be a fertile soil for both wheat and tares. One need not turn to the Freudian psychoanalysts to understand his type of mind.

For seven years (1490–1497) Luther attended the elementary school in Mansfeld. As he looked back upon those years in later life, he often shuddered with horror at the punishments inflicted there, and denounced the ignorance of the schoolmasters of the fifteenth century. But one must bear in mind that after the year 1520 he was too apt to paint the civilization of Roman Catholic countries in dark colors. He then believed that he had been emancipated from a realm of utter darkness. No wonder that the picture of his youth in Mansfeld appeared gloomy at times.

At the age of fourteen he was sent to Magdeburg, where he was taught by some of the Brethren of the Common Life in the Cathedral School. These pious brethren no doubt exhorted him to read the Bible, for such was their custom wherever they went. They stressed the need of inner piety, vital faith, and true love, the love of God and man, as taught by Jesus and Paul. They must have helped increase Luther's religious ardor, but cannot have prepared his mind for heresy.

In the year 1498 Luther went to Eisenach, where he was kindly treated by the wife of a prosperous burgher, named Ursula Cotta. In school he made friends with the rector and one of the assistants. He received careful training in Latin grammar, rhetoric, and poetry, so that when in 1501 he left Eisenach to enter the University of Erfurt, he had received an adequate secondary course of studies.

Erfurt was said to be the most populous place in Germany, but it is probable that cities like Cologne, Nuremberg, and Lübeck were a trifle larger, and that the population of Erfurt scarcely exceeded 25,000. The University at this time was not surpassed by any other institution of learning in German lands, while the numerous churches and monasteries lent a religious air to the city that was hardly equalled anywhere outside of Italy. Erfurt was aptly termed a "little Rome." It was in this city that Luther became a scholar and a monk.

Luther's reminiscences of his student life in Erfurt are not altogether favorable. He complains of the laxity in morals and of the amazing indolence so common among students at that time. And even though the critic must bear in mind how prone Luther was later to condemn the institutions which linked him with Catholicism, nevertheless he will have to grant that medieval universities were corrupt in many ways.

Luther experienced little difficulty in passing the course which led up to the degree of Master of Arts. Among the seventeen candidates which appeared for examination in 1505, the sturdy youth from Mansfeld secured second place. It is not true that Luther despised his teachers, nor did he seem to be rebellious, obstinate, or excessively melancholy. The chief subjects in his curriculum were naturally philosophy and theology. Since the professors were disciples of Occam, Luther became a sworn defender of the Occamist school of philosophy.

Aristotle's works were the chief sources of information for university students. Luther eagerly imbibed the teachings of the venerated Greek scholar. At Erfurt, he said later, he "read diligently the works of Aristotle, and because Aristotle observes the right method, he is to be highly esteemed." But he also said this: "Aristotle knows nothing of the soul, of God, and of immortality." In other words, Aristotle remained in Luther's mind a great authority on metaphysics, ethics, and dialectics, but not a reliable guide in the realm of theology.

Luther had his doubts about various accepted dogmas and customs, but they were usually silenced in quick order. Occam had attacked the papal authority when the contest between the pope and emperor was waging, but Luther did not evince much interest in political issues. John of Wesel, a former professor at Erfurt, and regarded as a heretic afterward, did not impress Luther as a theologian. Luther showed no signs of becoming a critic and a reformer. And for many years after he left the University, he remained as ardent a Roman Catholic as he had been before.

Now that Luther had secured his degree, he was expected to teach in the University for a period of two years. Acting upon a wish of his father that he become a lawyer, he also took up the study of law. He did not continue this study very long, for within two months he suddenly decided to enter a monastery. His motives have never been clear to all biographers. Some claim that the young man was bound to experience this crisis sooner or later. Imbued with a deep-seated terror of God and Christ as inexorable judges of mankind, he is supposed to have seen no issue but recourse to the monastic life. There is not enough evidence available, however, to prove this contention. A careful study of the sources will result in the belief that Luther's decision was not premeditated. On July 2nd he was overtaken by a terrific thunderstorm. Invoking St. Anna, he vowed to become a monk, and once having made the vow, he felt obliged to keep it. Two weeks later he bade his friends farewell. On July 17th he entered the Augustinian monastery. Thus ended the first period in his life, a period which unfortunately has not been illuminated with many reliable records. Luther's experiences after July, 1505, are on the contrary more numerous and far more reliable, so that the following selection may be expected to require no further introduction.

DATA ON THE SOURCES

There is probably no problem in the whole history of modern Europe which necessitates the use of as much caution in studying the sources as is the case with the theological development of Luther from 1505 till 1530. In the first place one will have to make a careful distinction between the authentic works of Luther and those which were either partly or entirely written down by others. One must also bear in mind that Luther himself did not always recall exactly what had happened to him in earlier years. Again, the Reformer frequently exaggerated, unconsciously or otherwise, the corruption in the Church that he had witnessed. The difficulties increase when the critic approaches the accounts left by contemporaries. And finally, the printed editions are not in all cases accurate. Much, therefore, will depend on the interpretation of the sources; perhaps even more in the present study on the method of selection.

I. LUTHER'S WORKS

1. O. Scheel, *Dokumente zu Luthers Entwicklung*, Tübingen, 1911. This is the most convenient source book for the study of Luther's theological development up to 1519. It gives 326 selected sources, mostly from Luther's works.

2. *Luthers Werke, Kritische Gesamtausgabe*, Weimar, 1883 ff. This impressive set of over 60 volumes is still in

the course of publication. It has for the most part super-
seded the Erlangen edition, but the first volumes have not
been properly edited. The Weimar edition contains much
material which had never been published before, such as
Luther's first sermons, his marginal notes on the *Sentences*
of Lombard, some treatises of Augustine, and a number of
sermons by Tauler, which he studied between 1509 and
1515; and finally, a complete edition of his lectures on the
Psalms (1513–1515).

3. *Luther's Letters,* edited by L. Enders and G. Kawerau,
1884 ff. Thus far 18 volumes have appeared, of which the
last two by P. Fleming and O. Albrecht. Useful is the English translation of Luther's most important letters by Pre-
served Smith, 2 vols.; Philadelphia, 1913, 1918. Also the
volume by M. A. Currie, London, 1908.

4. J. Ficker, *Luthers Volesung Über den Römerbrief
1515–16,* Leipzig, 1908; containing an introduction of 102
pages and the annotated text of Luther's *Lectures on the
Epistle to the Romans,* based on the autograph manuscript
of Luther now in the State Library at Berlin. This work
is an extremely important source, as it contains the first
presentation of Luther's changed view on the doctrine of
justification by faith.

5. *Luther's German Translation of the Bible,* 4 vols.,
numbered separately in the Weimar edition of Luther's
works, under the title of *Die Deutsche Bibel.*

6. *Luther's Table Talks,* 6 vols., numbered separately in
the Weimar edition of Luther's works, under the title of
Tischreden. Another volume of the *Tischreden,* or *Table
Talks,* is that by Johann Schlaginhaufen, entitled *Tischreden Luthers aus den Jahren 1531 und 1532,* and was edited
by W. Preger, Leipzig, 1888.

7. O. Clemen, *Luthers Werke in Auswahl,* 4 vols., Bonn,

1912–1913. This set contains some of the more important works by Luther, edited with superior care.

II. INDIRECT OR SECONDARY SOURCES

8. Melanchthon, *Preface to the Second Volume of Luther's Works,* Wittenberg, 1546. This preface contains a biographical sketch in Latin, which was reprinted in the *Corpus Reformatorum,* vol. VI, col. 155–170. A good deal of it is unreliable. More valuable are his letters and treatises, published in the same set.

9. Paul Luther, *On the Experiences of Luther in Rome,* printed in J. Köstlin, *Martin Luther,* vol. I, p. 749, and reprinted in Scheel's *Dokumente,* p. 2. This source used to be accepted by many writers, but Luther's own words discredit the account of his son Paul.

10. Crotus Rubianus, *Letter to Luther,* dated October 16, 1519, published in E. Böcking, *Hutteni Opera,* vol. I, Leipzig, 1859, pp. 309–311. Crotus was a fellow-student of Luther in the University of Erfurt.

11. D. Erasmus, *Letters,* published in the Latin original by P. S. Allen; thus far five volumes have appeared. The title is *Opus Epistolarum Des, Erasmi Roterodami,* Oxford. 1906 ff.

12. B. J. Kidd, *Documents Illustrative of the Continental Reformation,* Oxford, 1911. This volume contains a copy of Luther's 95 *Theses,* the Papal Bull *Exurge Domine,* Luther's *Answer Before the Diet of Worms,* the *Short Catechism* of Luther, and the *Augsburg Confession;* besides these a large number of other sources.

THE SOURCES

1. Luther, *Dedication for the De Votis Monasticis,* in: *Werke,* III, 573–574. Written in 1521, addressed to his father.

   I was called to this vocation by the terrors of heaven, for neither willingly nor by my own desire did I become a monk, but, surrounded by the terror and agony of a sudden death, I vowed a forced and unavoidable vow.

2. Luther, *Letter to Melanchthon,* September 9, 1521. Enders edition, III, 225.

   I was forced rather than drawn into making this vow.

3. Luther, *Tischreden,* IV, 440; Scheel, *Dokumente,* no. 30. Dated July 16, 1539.

   When I had been on my way for fourteen days and was near Stotternheim, not far from Erfurt, I became frightened by a flash of lightning, and exclaimed: "Help me, dear Saint Anna, I wish to become a monk." Later I repented of my vow, and many tried to dissuade me from keeping it, but I persevered.

4. Luther, *Tischreden,* IV, 303. Dated March 18, 1539. Scheel, *Dokumente,* no. 31.

God let me become a monk in order that I, having been taught by experience, might write against the papacy. I was forced to become a monk against my father's will.

5. Crotus Rubianus, *Letter to Luther,* dated October 16, 1519; Scheel, *Dokumente,* no. 88.

Divine Providence saw fit, when you were returning from a visit to your parents, to throw you, like another Paul, to the ground by a flash from heaven.

6. Ph. Melanchthon, *Vita M. Lutheri,* in *Corpus Reformatorum,* VI, 158. Dated 1546.

Luther suddenly entered the monastery, without consulting his parents and friends.

7. Luther, *Tischreden,* IV, 303.

For I made the vow not for the sake of the belly, but for the sake of my salvation.

8. Scheel, *Dokumente,* no. 19, giving an extract from one of Luther's sermons delivered in 1544.

When I became a monk, my father was about to go mad. He was greatly displeased, and did not want to give his consent. When I wrote him, he answered me, calling me *Du,* whereas before this he had called me *Ihr,* because of my Master's degree. Then came a pestilence, which robbed him of two of his sons. He was urged to make a holy sacrifice and give his consent to my entrance into the monastery. Father hesitated a long time, till finally he yielded. However, he did not do it willingly, with a free and happy heart.

II. Life in the Monastery

9. Luther observes the canonical regulations as prescribed in the constitution of the Observantine section of the Augustinian Order of Mendicant Monks. Luther, *Commentary on the Gospel of John, ch. VI–VIII*. Weimar edition, XXXIII, 561. Dated October 21, 1531.

I was an earnest monk, lived strictly and chastely, would not have taken a penny without the knowledge of the prior, prayed diligently day and night.

10. Same source, vol. XXXIII, p. 574. Dated October 28, 1531.

I kept vigil night by night, fasted, prayed, chastised and mortified my body, was obedient, and lived chastely.

11. Luther, *Answer to Duke George's latest Book,* Weimar edition, XXXVIII, 143. Scheel, *Dokumente,* no. 61. Dated 1533.

It is true that I have been a pious monk, and followed my rules so strictly that I may say, if ever a monk could have gained heaven through monkery, I should certainly have got there. This all my fellow-monks who have known me will attest.

12. Luther, *Letter to Jerome Weller,* dated 1530. Enders edition, VIII, 159–160.

Soon after my entrance into the monastery, I was always sad and could not free myself from this sadness.

13. Luther, *Exposition of Psalm XLV,* Erlangen edition, XVIII, 226; Scheel, *Dokumente,* no. 65.

When I was a monk, I exhausted myself by fasting, watching, praying, and other fatiguing labors. I seriously believed that I could secure justification through my works, and I could not have believed it possible that I would abandon this kind of life.

14. Luther, *Commentary on Paul's Epistle to the Galatians,* Erlangen edition, I, 109, 107. Scheel, *Dokumente,* no. 53, no. 55. Dated 1535.

My whole life was little more than fasting, watching, prayers, sighs, etc. But beneath this cover of sanctity and this confidence in my own justification, I felt a continued doubt, a fear, a desire to hate and blaspheme God.

Before the light of the Gospel, I was attached to the papal laws and the traditions of the Fathers. With all the zeal of which I was capable, I forced myself to observe them in fasting, watching, prayers, and other exercises; and mortified my body more than they who now hate me so violently and persecute me, because I take from them the glory of self-justification. I was so zealous and so superstitious that I imposed more on my body than it could bear without endangering my health.

15. Luther, *Sermon on Matthew XVIII–XXIV*, Erlangen edition, XLV, 156. Scheel, *Dokumente*, no. 27. Dated 1539.

In the monastery we had enough to eat and to drink, but we suffered martyrdom in our hearts. The greatest suffering is that of the soul. I was often frightened by the name of Jesus, and when I looked at him hanging on the cross, I fancied that he seemed to me like lightning. When I heard his name mentioned, I would rather have heard the name of the devil, for I thought that I had to perform good works until at last through them Jesus would become merciful to me. In the monastery I did not think about money, nor worldly possessions, nor women, but my heart shuddered when I wondered when God should become merciful to me.

III. THE VISIT TO ROME, DEC. 1510–JAN. 1511

16. Paul Luther believes that his father was converted in Rome. Scheel, *Dokumente*, no. 2. Dated 1582.

In the year 1544 did my father in the presence of his table companions and all of us tell the whole story of his trip to Rome, where he had to attend to some business affairs. Among other things he revealed with great pleasure that through the Holy Spirit he was made acquainted in Rome with the truth of the Gospel, and in the following manner. When he was saying his prayers on the steps of the Lateran Staircase, the verse from Habakkuk entered his mind, which Paul gives in the first chapter of the Epistle to the Romans, namely, "The just shall live by faith."

17. Luther contradicts the report of his son. Luther, *Predigt vom 24. Sonntag nach Trin. (November 15) 1545; Sermon on Paul's Epistle to the Col. I, 9 ff.* Printed in O. Scheel, *Dokumente; Nachträge* (1917), p. 10.

In Rome I wanted to deliver my grandfather from Purgatory, and I ascended the Staircase of Pilate, reciting on each step a "Pater noster." People said that he who prayed in this way would save a soul. But when I arrived at the top, I said to myself, "Who knows if it is true?"

18. Luther, *Tischreden,* Weimar edition, V, 181. Recorded by Kaspar Heydenreich.

Rome has become a courtesan. I would not accept 1000 florins (gulden) for not having seen Rome, for I could not have believed such a thing if some one had told me, and I had not seen it myself. People make fun of us there, because we were such pious monks, and they considered a Christian simply a fool.

19. Luther, *Dedication of the Commentary on Psalm XCVII,* Erlangen edition, XL, 284. Scheel, *Dokumente,* no. 79.

Since I was such a fanatical saint, I ran from one church to another, and believed all the lies that had been told there. I said about ten masses, and I was almost sorry that my father and mother were still living, for I would have loved to release them from Purgatory with my masses.

20. Luther, *Exposition of Matthew XXI,* in his *Works,* Weimar edition, XLVII, 392. Dated 1537–1540.

Whoever went to Rome and brought money with him, obtained the forgiveness of sins. I, like a fool, carried onions there and brought back garlic.

IV. LUTHER'S THEOLOGY BEFORE 1513

21. Luther, *Resolutiones super Propositionibus Suis Lipsia Disputatis,* Weimar edition, II, 414. Dated 1519.

I know and confess that I learned nothing from the scholastic theologians but ignorance of sin, righteousness, baptism, and the whole Christian life. Briefly, I not only learned nothing, but I learned only what I had to unlearn as contrary to the divine Scriptures.

22. The doctrine of predestination. Luther, *Letter to Count Albrecht of Mansfeld;* Scheel, *Dokumente,* no. 17. Dated December 8, 1542.

If your Highness is immersed in those doubts (namely, that predestination destroys all personal responsibility), I should be very sorry, for I also used to be troubled with them, and if Dr. Staupitz or rather God through Dr. Staupitz had not relieved me of them, I would have drowned in them, and have landed in hell long ago. For such devilish thoughts, where hearts are feeble, cause people to despair of God's mercy, and if they are brave, they will despise God, and become his enemies; and they will say, "Let things run their course, I shall act as I please, since everything is lost anyhow."

23. Staupitz (the head of the monastery) and Luther. J. Schlaginhaufen, *Tischreden Luthers aus den Jahren*

1531 und 1532, ed. W. Preger, no. 257. Dated April, 1532.

One day I complained to Staupitz that the doctrine of predestination was so enigmatical. He responded, "It is in the wounds of Christ that the meaning of predestination is found, and not anywhere else; for it is written: 'Hear Him' (Matt. XVII, 5). The Father is sublime, but he said, 'I will show you the way to come to me, that is to say, Christ. Go and believe in me, attach yourself to Christ, then you will find out in due time who I am.' This we are not doing, hence God to us is incomprehensible and unintelligible."

24. Same source, no. 56. Dated December, 1531.

When Philip left us, Luther said to me, Do not be afraid, you will get better, for I know that your temptations will add to the glory of God and to our well-being and that of many others. I have also lain sick in the hospital, but had no consoler. When I revealed my temptations to Staupitz, he said, "I don't understand it, I know nothing about it." Later I spoke to him about my temptations, when I was going to the altar. He responded, "Gerson and the other fathers have said that it is sufficient to remain in the first intention. Your first intention was to secure remission of sin."

25. Gerson's views on the nature of temptation. Same source as above, no. 119. Dated between January 1 and March 31, 1532.

Gerson is the only one who wrote of spiritual temptation, all the others knew only of physical temptation, such as

Jerome, Augustine, Ambrose, Bernard, Scotus, Thomas Aquinas, Richard of St. Victor, and Occam. Gerson was an excellent man, who was not a monk, but it did not happen to him that his conscience was consoled by Christ, but he wrote in extenuation of the law, "It cannot all be so very sinful," and so he was content to remain under the law.

26. Luther experiences a spiritual conflict. N. Ericeus, *Sylvula Sententiarum*, 1566, pp. 174 ff. Scheel, *Dokumente*, no. 76. The same in Luther, *Tischreden*, I, 240.

I often confessed my troubles to Staupitz, and I did not speak to him about women, but about my real knotted problems. He said to me, "I do not understand." That was a fine consolation! When I addressed others, I received the same answer. No confessor cared to know anything about it. Then I said to myself, Nobody experiences this temptation but you. I was almost a corpse. Finally Staupitz said to me at the table, seeing how sad and crestfallen I was, "Why are you so sad?" I answered, What will become of me? "You don't know," he continued, "how necessary such a trial is to you. Without it you will not be worth anything." He did not understand. He thought I was learned, and was becoming proud.

27. Luther, *Letter to Staupitz*, May 20, 1518. Enders, I, 196–197.

I recall, reverend father, that in your agreeable and salutary remarks, in which Jesus used to console me so admirably, the subject of penitence was discussed one day. We were full of compassion for those consciences which were martyred by the executioners, who invented innumerable and insufferable precepts for those who go to confess their sins. The word you spoke seemed to me to have come from

heaven: "True repentance begins with the love of justice
and of God." That which according to others constitutes
the end and consummation of repentance is on the contrary the beginning. That word stuck in me as the sharp
arrow of a warrior, and I began to compare it with the
words of Scripture concerning penitence. And what was
my surprise! From all sides the biblical words confirmed
your opinion. Whereas formerly there was no more bitter
word in the Bible than penitence, now no word seemed
sweeter to me than that of penitence. For it is thus that the
precepts of God become sweet, when we learn to read them,
not only in books, but in the very sweet wounds of the
Savior.

28. Luther, *Letter to John Braun in Eisenach*, March 17,
     1509. Enders, I, 6.

Now I am at Wittenberg, by God's command or permis-
sion. If you wish to know my condition, I am well by
the grace of God, except that my studies are severe, especially philosophy, which from the beginning I would have
gladly exchanged for theology,—that theology which goes
to the kernel of the nut and touches the bone and the flesh.
But God is God; man often, if not always, errs in his
judgment. He is our God, who will guide us lovingly to
all eternity.

V. The Lectures on the Psalms (1513–1515)

LUTHER'S *WERKE*, WEIMAR EDITION, VOLS. III AND IV

29. Man is corrupt. Vol. III, 462.

All that is in us and in the world is abominable and damnable in the presence of God, and thus he who adheres to

him through faith necessarily appears to himself vile and nothing, abominable and damnable.

30. Justification. Vol. III, 345, 388, 31, 29, 31.

No one can be justified by faith unless he has first confessed through humility that he is unjust. . . .

We are all sinners and cannot become righteous except through faith in Christ. . . .

The righteousness of God cannot arise within us until our righteousness entirely falls and perishes. . . .

The just man falls seven times and rises again each time. It is impossible that he who has confessed his sin is not just, if he speaks the truth. Where Christ is, there is truth. But since the remission of sin is the resurrection of the sinners, it follows that sin will not be forgiven to sinners when they do not accuse themselves: hence they will not rise again nor be justified. . . .

What our scholastic theologians call the act of penance, namely to be displeased with oneself, to detest, to condemn, to accuse oneself,—that with one word the Scripture calls justification. Hence as long as we do not condemn ourselves before God, so long we shall neither rise nor be justified. Paul wants to be found in Christ, having no justification of his own (Phil. III, 9). Thus he calls himself the greatest of all sinners (I Tim. I, 15), which is a great and happy pride. For the more sin abounds, the more does the grace and justification of God abound in us (Rom. V, 20). In other words, the less justification we have of our own, the more abundantly does the grace of God flow into us.

31. The Old Law and the New. Vol. III, 37, 96.

All that is the letter of the law which only pertains to the body and the senses, and not to the spirit. And because all

things which are done under the law are only done exter-
nally and with the senses, they are called carnal and of the
letter and vain and not good, because they do not do any
good to the spirit. In the new law are given free and spiritual
gifts; and in the law those are removed which are carnal
and of the letter. . . .

The law which is known and observed literally is neither
pure nor holy, because it does not sanctify the soul. The law
is to be understood spiritually, like the gospel.

32. Vol. III, 171. Title of the lecture on Psalm XXXI
(XXXII).

Of the true way of doing penance, that sins are forgiven
through no works, but by the sole mercy of God who does
not impute them.

33. Vol. III, 172, 174.

The Apostle Paul speaks against all those who wish to
have their sins forgiven by God through their works and
merits, and to be justified by their own works. Thus Christ
would have died in vain, because they would be saved by
their own works, without the death of Christ, which is
false. . . .

No one is blessed, unless his iniquity has been forgiven
him. Hence no one is without iniquity, no one is not the son
of wrath and makes efforts to have his iniquity remitted.
This is not done except through Christ, hence no one is saved
by himself, but only by Christ. And this is also the conclusion of the whole Epistle of Paul to the Romans. For he
says, "The righteousness of God is revealed therein," etc.
(Rom. I, 17). It signifies: no man knows that the wrath of
God abides upon all men and that all are in sin in his sight,
but through his Gospel God reveals from Heaven how we

shall be saved from that wrath, and through which righteousness we shall be delivered, namely through Christ.

34. Vol. III, 155, 122.

It is to be feared that all Observantines, all exempted, all privileged monks, must be reckoned among those puffed up in their carnal mind. How harmful they are to the Church has not yet become clear, but the fact remains and will make itself apparent in time. If we ask why they insist upon isolation, they reply, "On account of the protection of the cloistral discipline." But that is the light of an angel of Satan. . . .

The fate of divine condemnation will fall upon all the proud and the stiff-necked, all the superstitious, rebellious, disobedient; also, as I fear, on our Observantines, who under a show of strict discipline are only loading themselves with insubordination and rebellion.

35. Vol. III, 424–425.

Popes and bishops are flinging about graces and indulgences. Here come religious men and flaunt their indulgences at every street corner, only to get money for food and clothing. Oh, those begging friars!

VI. Luther Breaks with the Theology of the Roman Catholic Church, as Indicated by his Lectures on Paul's Epistle to the Romans (1515–1516)

36. Part II, 243.

The Pope and the chief pastors of the Church have become corrupt and their works deserving of malediction;

they stand forth today as seducers of the Christian people.

37. Part II, 275, 317.

We busy ourselves with trivialities, build churches, increase the possessions of the Church, heap money together, multiply the ornaments and vessels of silver and gold in the churches, erect organs and the pomps which please the eye. We make piety consist in this. But where is the man who sets himself to carry out the Apostle's exhortations, not to speak of the great prevailing vices of pride, arrogance, avarice, immorality, and ambition. . . .

It is necessary that Fast days be done away with and many of the Feast days be abrogated. Almost the whole of the Christian Code ought to be purified and changed, and the pomp, ceremonies, devotions, and adorning of the churches reduced.

38. Part II, 301.

The horrible corruption of the papal curia and the mountain of the most terrible immorality, pomp, avarice, ambition, and sacrilege is accounted no sin.

39. Part II, 110, 167, 108.

They are delirious who say that man by his own power can love God above all things. O proud, O hoggish theologians! . . .

The scholastic doctors talk obscurely and neither plainly nor intelligibly, saying that no deed under the law has any value unless formed by love. Cursed be the phrase "formed of love," and the distinction between works according to the substance of the deed and the intention of the Law-giver. . . .

In their arbitrary fashion they assert that on the infusion of Grace the whole of original sin is remitted in every one just as all actual sin, as though sin could thus be removed at once, in the same way as darkness is dispelled by light. It is true their Aristotle made sin and righteousness to consist in works. Either I never understood them, or they did not express themselves well.

40. Part II, 273.

The very word righteousness vexes me. It is a word which the jurists always have on their lips, but there is no more unlearned race than these men of the law, save, per-haps, the men of good intention and superior wisdom.

41. Man has no free will. Part II, 212, 209, 322.

Free will apart from grace possesses absolutely no power for righteousness. Therefore St. Augustine in his book against Julian terms it "rather an enslaved than a free will." But after the obtaining of grace it becomes really free, at least as far as salvation is concerned. The will is, it is true, free by nature, but only for what comes within its province, not for what is above it, being bound in the chain of sin and therefore unable to choose what is good in God's sight. . . .

Where is our righteousness, where are our works, where is the liberty of choice? This is what must be preached, this is the way to bring the wisdom of the flesh to the dust! The Apostle does so here. In former passages he cuts off its hands, its feet, its tongue; here he seizes it and makes an end of it. Here, like a flash of light, it is seen to possess nothing of itself, all its possession being in God. . . .

42. Part II, 183–184.

Man can of himself do nothing.

The fulfilling of the law through our own efforts is impossible; it cannot even be said that we have the power to will and to be able, in such a way as God would have us; for otherwise grace would not be necessary, and otherwise the sin of Adam would not have corrupted our motives or nature, but have left it unimpaired. Nature, by original sin, is blinded in its knowledge and chained in its affections, and therefore cannot know God, nor love him above all things nor yet refer all to him.

43. Part II, 111.

Everywhere in the Church great relapses after confession are now noticeable. People are confident that they are justified instead of first awaiting justification, and therefore the devil has an easy task with such false assurance of safety, and overthrows men. All this is due to making righteousness consist in works.

44. The nature and results of original sin, and the view expressed by Gerard Zerbolt, whom Luther wrongly called Gerard Groote. Part II, 143–145.

And what is original sin? According to the subtle arguments of the scholastic theologians, it is the absence of original justice. According to the Apostle and the simple teachings of Jesus Christ, it is not merely the deprivation of a function in the will, not merely the withdrawal of light from the intellect, or power from the memory, but it is the loss of all rectitude and all efficacy in all our faculties, both of the body and the soul, of the interior and the whole of the exterior man. It is besides the inclination to do evil, the dislike of good, the aversion to light and wisdom, the love of error and darkness, the departure from and abomination of good works, and the approach of evil. Hence, as the Fathers have justly remarked, this original sin is the fuel itself of concupiscence, the law of the flesh, the law of the members, the disease of nature, the tyrant, the original disease. Here you have that hydra with its many heads, that imperishable monster with which we here below are struggling till death. Here you have that untamable Cerberus, that invincible Antæos. I have found no one to give such a clear explanation of original sin as Gerard Groote in his little treatise: "Blessed is the Man," where he does not speak as a rash philosopher, but as a sound theologian.

45. Gerard Zerbolt's view on original sin. *De Spiritualibus Ascensionibus,* which begins with "Blessed is the man," Chapter III.

We have been contaminated by original sin, and wounded in all the powers and faculties of the soul. For through the loss of original justice as a result of our fall and the just judgments of God, these powers and feelings, having fallen from their proper status, have become deranged and diminished, though not completely destroyed. Hence it happens that these powers and feelings deviate from their proper course, instituted by God; they are prone to evil. Again, our reason, rendered vacillating and obtuse, often accepts falsehood for truth, and frequently busies itself with useless and vain thoughts. The will has become warped; it often chooses degenerate objects, loves carnal, and detests spiritual and celestial things. Our desires are deformed: they are covetous, and have degenerated into carnal lusts. Our hope does not seek God, but wealth and fame, or something it has no right to ask for. We are grieved by loss of temporal riches, and of honor. Christ through his precious death does indeed redeem us from our original sin, so that this loss of soul powers or the law of the flesh is not guilt, in order that there be no condemnation for those who are in Jesus Christ; though he does not at once restore us to our original righteousness, nor does Christ reform the faculties of our soul, but left those to be reformed by us through saintly exercises.

46. Luther's views on sins committed after baptism and confession. Part II, 178.

Sin, therefore, remains in the spiritual man for his exercise in the life of grace, for the humbling of his pride, for the driving back of his presumptions. Whoever does not exert himself zealously in the struggle against it, is in danger of being condemned, even though he cease to sin any more. We must carry on a war with our desires, for they are culpable, they are really sins and render us worthy of damnation; only the mercy of God does not impute them to us when we fight manfully against them, calling upon God's grace.

47. Luther's own experiences with sin. Part II, 108–109.

Thus I, fool that I was, could not understand how I ought to repute myself a sinner and prefer myself to no one after I was repentant and had confessed my sin. For I thought that all sin had been removed and evacuated even intrinsically. But if past sin is to be called to mind, then, thought I, these sins have not been removed, though God has promised their remission to those who confess. Thus I fought with myself, not knowing that there is truly remission, but nevertheless not the removal of sin, but only the hope that it will be taken away and the grace of God given, which begins to take it away in the sense that it is not imputed as sin.

48. Divine Providence. Part II, 208.

With God there is absolutely no chance, but only with us; for no leaf ever falls from a tree to the earth without the will of the Father.

49. Predestination. Part II, 213–217.

God commands that the elect shall be saved and that those who are destined for hell shall be entangled in evil in order that he may show forth his mercy and also his anger. . . .

Man must learn that his salvation does not depend on his acts, but that it is quite outside of him, namely, in God, who has chosen him. . . .

To them who love God, with filial love, which is not of nature but only of the Holy Spirit—to them these words (Rom. IX, 3) are most excellent. They submit themselves to the whole will of God, even to hell and external damnation, if God should want that. However, if they wholly conform to the will of God, it is impossible that they should remain in hell.

50. Justification. Part II, 14, 121, 33–34, 104.

The righteousness by which God justifies, differs from that of man, which is concerned with works. According to Aristotle in the third book of *Ethics,* righteousness follows and arises from man's acts. According to God it precedes work and works arise from it. For just as no one can do the works of a bishop or a priest unless he is first consecrated for the purpose, so no one can do righteous works unless he first becomes righteous. . . .

Righteousness and unrighteousness are understood very differently in Scripture from what the philosophers and the jurists understand by these words. For they assert that it is a quality of the soul. But the righteousness of Scripture depends more on the imputation of God than on the essence of the thing. For in the Scripture he has not righteousness who has only the quality of it; yea, such a one is a sinner and altogether unrighteous, and only he is righteous whom God, on account of the confession of his unrighteousness, and his imploring the divine righteousness, mercifully reputes and wills to esteem righteous. . . .

God does not freely give grace in the sense that he exacts no satisfaction for sin. But he gave Christ as the satisfier on our behalf in order that he might freely give grace to those who thus themselves make satisfaction through another, and that we, being unrighteous, should seek our righteousness from God alone, who first remits our sins on account of Christ's propitiatory suffering. . . .

We are righteous extrinsically and not of ourselves, or our works, but solely by the imputation of God.

51. Part II, 103–104, 221.

God does not accept the person on account of the works, but the works on account of the person. . . .

How can a man boast of his own merits and works, which are in no way pleasing to God because they are good and meritorious, but because God has decided from eternity that they shall be pleasing to him? Our works do not make us good, but the goodness of God makes us good and our works good.

52. Part II, 105, 86, 234.

We must, believing in the word of the cross, die to ourselves and to everything; then we shall live for God alone. . . .

The faith in Christ, by which we will be justified, is to be a faith not only in Christ, or in the person of Christ, but we must believe everything that is of Christ. . . .

Faith is life, and the living word abbreviated. . . .

Unless faith illumines and love frees, no man is able to will, or possess, or work anything good.

53. Part II, 214, 124.

Those who fear and tremble about their election have the best token of it. For in despairing of themselves, the Word of God which produces this fear does its own work. . . .

As God and his counsel are unknown to us, so is our righteousness, which wholly depends on him and his counsel.

54. Part I, 20; Part II, 107–108, 113, 178–179.

Only the doers of the law will be justified in the sight of God. . . .

It is with the believer as with the sick man who believes the physician which promises him most certain recovery, and who, obeying the precept in the hope of this promised restoration, abstains from those things which the physician prohibits, lest he hinder his recovery and aggravate the disease, until the physician fulfills his promise. Is this sick man then healthy? He is indeed at the same time sick and healthy. He is sick in reality, but healthy by the certain promise of the physician whom he believes, who reputes him sound, because he is certain that he will heal him. In the same way Christ takes the half-dead man, his sick one, into his hospital for the purpose of curing him, and begins to heal him, promising him the most perfect restoration to eternal life. . . .

The justified person is already converted and pious, and he worships God and seeks him in fear and hope. . . .

Sin remains in the spiritual man for the exercise of grace, for the humbling of pride, and the repression of presumption. For we are not called to ease, but to labor against the passions.

VII. LUTHER AND THE *THEOLOGICA GERMANICA* (1516–1517)

55. Luther, *Letter to Spalatin*, December 14, 1516. Enders, I, 75.

If you delight in reading pure, sound theology, like that of the earliest age, and in German, read the sermons of John Tauler, of the Order of the Dominicans [1] of whose

---

[1] The author of this *Theologica* is not Tauler, but probably a member of the brotherhood of the Friends, a group of mystics who lived in Western Germany.

teaching I send you herewith an epitome. For I have not found in Latin or German a more wholesome theology, or one more consonant with the Gospel. Taste, therefore, and see how sweet is the Lord, where formerly you have seen how bitter is everything in us.

56. Luther, *Werke,* Weimar edition, I, 378–379.

Let anyone who wishes to read this little book do so, and then say whether our theology is new or old. I thank God that I thus hear and find my God in the German tongue, as I and they along with me, have not hitherto found either in Latin, Greek, or Hebrew.

57. Extracts from the *Theologica Germanica.* Chapters III, XIV.

In this restoration and recovery I can, may, and shall do nothing, but simply yield myself so that God alone may do and work all things in me. . . .
Likewise Saint Paul says, "As in Adam all die, even so in Christ shall all men be made alive." Hence all of Adam's children are dead in God's sight. As long as man is in disobedience, his sin can never be atoned; do whatever he will, it avails him nothing.

VIII. LUTHER AND THE HUMANISTS (1516–1517)

58. The *Epistolae Obscurorum Virorum.* Luther, *Letter to John Lang,* October 5, 1516. Enders, I, 60.

It is quite clear that the nonsense you sent me about a supplication to the pope against "theologians" has been cooked up by some rash person, for it smells of the same oven as the *Epistolae Obscurorum Virorum.*

59. Luther, *Letter to George Spalatin,* October 5, 1516. Enders, I, 62.

John Lang, prior at Erfurt, has sent me the *Supplication Against Theologians.* As it contains no manifest truth, it must be by the author of the *Epistolae Obscurorum Virorum,* or someone who apes him.

60. Erasmus. Luther, *Letter to George Spalatin,* October 19, 1516. Enders I, 63.

What displeases me in Erasmus is that in interpreting Paul on the righteousness of works, or of the law, or our own righteousness, as the Apostle calls it, he understands only those ceremonial and figurative observances. I do not hesitate to disagree with Erasmus, because in interpreting the Scriptures I consider Jerome as much inferior to Augustine as Erasmus judges him superior.

61. Luther, *Letter to John Lang,* March 1, 1517. Enders, I, 88.

I have read our Erasmus, and my opinion of him grows daily worse. I am indeed pleased that he refutes stoutly and learnedly both the monks and the priests, and condemns their inveterate ignorance. But I fear that he does not advance sufficiently the cause of Christ and the grace of God, in which he is more ignorant than Lefèvre. The human weighs more with him than the divine. It seems to me that not everyone who knows Greek and Hebrew is for that reason a Christian, since Jerome, who knew five languages, did not equal Augustine, who knew but one, although Erasmus thinks Jerome superior. The opinion of him who attributes something to free will, is very different from the opinion of one who knows nothing but grace.

62. Lefèvre. Luther, *Letter to Spalatin,* October 19, 1516. Enders, I, 64.

Even Lefèvre, a man otherwise spiritual and sincere, lacks this proper understanding of the Scriptures when he interprets them, although he has it abundantly in his own life and in exhorting others.

63. Christopher Scheurl to John Eck at Ingolstadt, January 14, 1517. Translation in P. Smith, *Luther's Correspondence,* vol. I, Philadelphia, 1913, no. 29.

Among the theologians at Wittenberg the most eminent are Martin Luther, the Augustinian, who expounds the epistles of Paul with marvelous genius, Carlstadt, Amsdorff, Feltkirchen, and others.

IX. LUTHER'S ATTACK ON THE SALE OF INDULGENCES
(1517–1518)

64. The Ninety-five theses posted on the door of the castle church in Wittenberg, October 31, 1517. Printed in Luther's *Works,* Weimar edition, I, 233–238. See also O. Clemen, *Luthers Werke in Auswahl,* vol. I, Bonn, 1912, pp. 3–9. A good English translation is found in H. Wace and C. A. Buchheim, *First Principles of the Reformation,* London, 1883, pp. 6–13. This translation was used for the following selection.

Disputation of Dr. Martin Luther Concerning Penitence and Indulgences.

(1) Our Lord and Master Jesus Christ in saying: "Repent ye," etc., intended that the whole life of believers should be penitence.

(2) This word cannot be understood of sacramental penance, that is, of the confession and satisfaction which are performed under the ministry of priests.

(3) It does not, however, refer solely to inward penitence; nay such inward penitence is naught, unless it outwardly produces various mortifications of the flesh.

(4) The penalty thus continues as long as the hatred of self—that is, true inward penitence—continues, namely, till our entrance into the kingdom of heaven.

(5) The Pope has neither the will nor the power to remit any penalties, except those which he has imposed by his own authority, or by that of the canons.

(6) The Pope has no power to remit any guilt, except by declaring and warranting it to have been remitted by God; or at most by remitting cases reserved for himself; in which cases, if his power were despised, guilt would certainly remain.

(7) God never remits any man's guilt, without at the same time subjecting him, humbled in all things, to the authority of his representative the priest.

(8) The penitential canons are imposed only on the living, and no burden ought to be imposed on the dying, according to them.

(9) Hence the Holy Spirit acting in the Pope does well

for us in that in his decrees he always makes exception of the article of death and of necessity.

(10) Those priests act wrongly, and unlearnedly, who, in the case of the dying, reserve the canonical penances for purgatory.

(11) Those tares about changing of the canonical penalty into the penalty of purgatory seem surely to have been sown while the bishops were asleep.

(12) Formerly the canonical penalties were imposed not after, but before absolution, as tests of true contrition.

(13) The dying pay all penalties by death, and are already dead to the canon laws, and are by right relieved from them.

(14) The imperfect vigor or charity of a dying person necessarily brings with it great fear, and the less it is, the greater the fear it brings.

(15) This fear and horror is sufficient by itself, to say nothing of other things, to constitute the pains of purgatory, since it is very near to the horror of despair.

(16) Hell, purgatory, and heaven appear to differ as despair, almost despair, and peace of mind differ.

(17) With souls in purgatory, it seems that it must needs be that, as horror diminishes, so charity increases.

(18) Nor does it seem to be proved by any reasoning, or any Scriptures, that they are outside of the state of merit or of the increase of charity.

(19) Nor does this appear to be proved, that they are sure and confident of their own blessedness, at least all of them, though we may be very sure of it.

(20) Therefore the Pope, when he speaks of the plenary

remission of all penalties, does not mean simply of all, but only of those imposed by himself.

(21) Thus those preachers of indulgences are in error who say that, by the indulgences of the Pope, a man is loosed and saved from all punishment.

(22) For in fact he remits to souls in purgatory no penalty which they would have had to pay in this life according to the canons.

(23) If any entire remission of all penalties can be granted to anyone, it is certain that it is granted to none but the most perfect, that is, to very few.

(24) Hence the greater part of the people must needs be deceived by this indiscriminate and high-sounding promise of release from penalties.

(25) Such power as the Pope has over purgatory in general, such is the power that every bishop has in his own diocese, and every curate in his own parish, in particular.

(26) The Pope acts most rightly in granting remission to souls, not by the power of the Keys (which is of no avail in this case) but by the way of intercession.

(27) They preach that a man's soul flies out (of purgatory) as soon as his money rattles in the chest.

(28) It is certain that, when the money rattles in the chest, avarice and gain may be increased, but the effect of the intercession of the Church depends on the will of God alone.

(36) Every Christian who feels true compunction has of right plenary remission of punishment and guilt even without letters of pardon.

(56) The treasures of the Church, whence the Pope

grants indulgences, are neither sufficiently named nor known among the people of Christ.

(57) It is clear that they are at least not temporal treasures, for these are not so readily lavished, but only accumulated, by many of the preachers.

(58) Nor are they the merits of Christ and of the saints, for these, independently of the Pope, are always working grace to the inner man, and the cross, death, and hell to the outer man.

(89) Since it is the salvation of souls, rather than money, that the Pope seeks by his pardons, why does he suspend the letters and pardons granted long ago, since they are equally efficacious?

(90) To repress these scruples and arguments of the laity by force alone, and not to solve them by giving reasons, is to expose the Church and the Pope to the ridicule of their enemies, and to make Christian men unhappy.

(91) If then pardons were preached according to the spirit and mind of the Pope, all these questions would be solved with ease; nay, would not exist.

(92) Away then with all those prophets who say to the people of Christ: "Peace, peace," and there is no peace.

(93) Blessed be all those prophets, who say to the people of Christ: "The Cross, the Cross," and there is no cross.

(94) Christians should be exhorted to strive to follow Christ, their head, through pains, deaths, and hells.

(95) And thus trust to enter heaven through many tribulations rather than in the security of peace.

65. Luther's attitude towards the 95 theses. L*etter to Christopher Scheurl,* March 5, 1518. Enders, I, 166.

I did not wish to have my theses widely circulated. I merely intended to submit them to a few learned men for examination, and if they approved of them, to suppress them. As yet I am still uncertain as to some points. I purpose issuing a book on the use and misuse of indulgences. I have no longer any doubt that the people are deceived, not through the indulgences, but through using them.

66. Extracts from the *Sermon on Indulgences,* April, 1518. Luther, *Eyn Sermon von dem Ablas,* in *Werke,* Weimar ed., I, 243–246.

Point seventeen. Indulgences are not commended, or urged, but belong to those things which are permitted. Hence they are not the fruit of obedience, nor meritorious. . . .
Point eighteen. I do not know whether souls are released from purgatory or not, and I do not believe it either. The Church has not settled that question. Hence it is better that you pray for it yourself, and act besides, for this is worth more and is sure.

67. Luther's attack grows more violent. Luther, *Resolutiones Disputationum de Indulgentiarum Virtute,* August, 1518. Printed in his *Works,* Weimar ed., I, 525–628. A better version appeared in Clemen's *Auswahl,* I, 16–147. It contains 95 conclusions, corresponding to the 95 theses. Some merely repeat the respective theses.

Conclusion I. Since Christ is Master of the spirit and not of the letter, and his words are life and spirit, it follows that he teaches that penitence which is felt in spirit and truth; not that penitence which the proud hypocrites can exhibit in fasting, praying, and giving alms. . . .

Conclusion II. Sacramental penance is temporal. It is external, and has its prerequisite in the word penance, without which it is of no value. This internal penance is possible without the sacramental penance. . . .

Conclusion LVIII. From these and many other facts, which would require too much space to enumerate here, I conclude that the merits of the saints are not greater than they need themselves. I am ready to suffer fire and death for these conclusions.

68. Luther and Cardinal Cajetan. Luther, *Letter to Andreas Carlstadt,* October 14, 1518. Enders, I, 249 (247).

The legate is determined I shall not hold a public disputation. The keenest discussion has been over these two articles: First, that I said indulgence is not the treasury of merits of our Lord and Savior Christ,—and second, that the man going to the sacrament must believe.

X. LUTHER BREAKS WITH THE CHURCH (1517–1520)

69. Luther, *Letter to John Lang,* October, 1516. Enders, I, 54.

I know what Gabriel Biel says, and it is all very good, except when he speaks of grace, charity, hope, faith, and virtue. He is a Pelagian.

70. Luther still regards the followers of Hus in Bohemia as heretics. Luther, *Letter to Spalatin,* December 31, 1517. Enders, I, 135.

It was never my aim to call the veneration of saints superstitious, even when they are invoked for the most worldly causes. For this is what our neighbors the Beghards of Bohemia think.

71. Luther, *Letter to Spalatin,* January 18, 1518. Enders, I, 141.

There are many things in Erasmus which seem to me far from the knowledge of Christ.

72. Same source.

The Bible cannot be mastered by study or talent. You must rely solely on the influx of the Spirit.

73. Luther, *Letter to Staupitz,* March 31, 1518. Enders, I, 176.

Truly I have followed the theology of Tauler. I teach that man should trust in nothing save Jesus Christ only; not in their own prayers, or merits, or works.

74. Same source.

I read the scholastics with an open mind; I neither reject all that they say, nor approve all.

75. Luther, *Letter to J. Trutfetter,* May 9, 1518. Enders, I, 188.

I believe it is impossible to reform the Church unless the Canon Law, scholastic theology, philosophy, and logic, as

they are now taught, are completely eradicated. I daily ask
the Lord that the pure study of the Bible and the Fathers
may be restored.

76. Melanchthon arrives in Wittenberg. Luther, *Letter to
    John Lang,* September 16, 1518. Enders, I, 237.

The very learned and perfect Grecian Philip Melanchthon is teaching Greek here. He is a mere boy in years, but
he is not only a master of Greek and Latin, but of all the
learning to which they are keys.

77. Luther, *Letter to Melanchthon,* October 11, 1518. En-
    ders, I, 245.

Italy is, as Egypt was long ago, cast into palpable darkness, being entirely ignorant of Christ and all that apper-
tains to him.

78. Luther, *Letter to John Reuchlin,* December 14, 1518.
    Enders, I, 321, 322.

Those who have the cause of learning at heart have long
wished for one like you. The Lord has achieved through
you that the king of the sophists may learn to be more
slow and cautious in opposing sound theology, and Germany may breathe again through the teaching of the Holy
Scriptures, which, alas, for so many hundred years has
been smothered and suppressed. It was Philip Melanchthon,
whom I am proud to call my dearest friend, who persuaded
me to write.

79. Luther, *Letter to John Eck,* January 7, 1519. Enders,
    V, 4.

The reason why I preferred Tauler to the scholastics is that I learned more from him alone than from all the others.

80. Luther still professes loyalty to the Church. Luther, *Letter to Pope Leo X*, March 3, 1519. Enders, I, 444.

I declare before God that I have never had the slightest wish to attack the power of the Roman Church, or your Holiness, in any way. I gladly promise to let the question of indulgence drop, if my opponents will restrain their boastful, empty talk.

81. (Erasmus reports that Luther has led a blameless life.) Erasmus, *Letter to the Elector Frederic of Saxony*, April 14, 1519. P. S. Allen, *Opus Epistolarum Erasmi*, III, 527.

No one who knows Luther does not approve his life, since he is as far as possible from the suspicion of avarice or ambition; and blameless morals find favor even among heathens.

82. Erasmus, *Letter to Cardinal Thomas Wolsey*, May 18, 1519. Allen, III, 587.

Luther's life is approved by the unanimous consent of all. His character is so upright that even his enemies find no cause in it for slander.

83. Luther begins to show interest in the teachings of Hus. Wenzel Rozd'alousky, *Letter to Luther*, July 17, 1519. Enders, II, 79.

A certain organist, called James, told·us that you greatly desired the book of John Hus. So I am sending you his book on the Church.

84. Luther debates with John Eck in Leipzig, July 4, 14, 1519. Here he breaks with the Roman Catholic Church. *Disputatio Joh. Eccii et M. Lutheri Lipsiae habita.* Printed in Luther's *Works,* II, 250–383. The following extracts are found on pp. 304, 339, 308, 288.

Paul rejected the authority of Peter (Gal. II, 4–14). . . . A church council does not err; if it errs, it is not a church council. . . .
A church council cannot make a divine law which in itself is not a divine law. . . .
The Pope and the councils are men; hence they are to be judged according to the Scriptures.

85. Luther, *Letter to Spalatin,* July 20, 1519. Enders, II, 83–84.

I proved to Eck from the decisions of the Council of Constance that not all the articles condemned there were heretical and erroneous.

86. Luther, *Letter to Spalatin,* February, 1520. Enders, II, 345.

Thus far I have unconsciously held and taught all the doctrines of John Hus. John Staupitz has also taught them in like ignorance. In short, we are all Hussites without knowing it.

87. Luther, *Letter to Spalatin,* November 7, 1519. Enders, II, 225.

Although I know that our church believes in purgatory, I do not know that all Christians do. It is certain that no one is a heretic for not believing in purgatory.

88. Rome compared with Babylon. Luther, *Prologue to Epitoma Responsionis ad Martinum Luther,* in Luther's *Works,* Weimar edition, VI, 329.

Farewell, Rome the miserable, perverted, and blasphemer. The wrath of God has at last come to you, as you have merited it.

89. A definition of the true Church. Luther, *Von dem Papsttum zu Rom wider den hochberühmten Romanisten zu Leipzig.* Luther's *Works,* VI, 293, 292, 297, 321–322, 301; O. Clemen, *Luthers Werke in Augswahl,* I, 331, 330, 335, 358–359, 339. Luther wrote this treatise in May–June, 1520.

The church is composed of all those who live in the true faith, hope, and love, so that the essence, the life, and the nature of Christianity is not an assembly of bodies, but a union of hearts in the one faith, as St. Paul says: "One baptism, one faith, one savior." Even if the members live in a thousand different places, they form one spiritual community. . . .

They are invited by the faith in Christ, the invisible head, and not by the submission to the Pope at Rome, the visible head. . . .

The Scriptures speak only in one way about the essence of Christianity. . . .

The Church and the Christian population are united in the same way as the soul lives in the body. The soul can live without the body. . . .

I do not like to see anyone oppose the papal power. We must obey the Pope, even as we would the Turk, if his power were established over us. I do not want to see people formulate new doctrines and then call all the other Christians heretics, simply because they are not under the papal power. It is sufficient that we let the Pope remain Pope, but it is not necessary that for his sake God and his saints on earth are injured. Again, I wish to have the right to judge the actions of the Pope according to the Scriptures. He is to remain under Christ and be directed by the Holy Spirit. The Romanists place him above Christ, and make him an authority higher than the Scriptures, one who cannot err.

90. The papacy is a human institution. Luther, *Letter to Spalatin*, March 13, 1519. Enders, I, 450. 450.

I don't know whether the pope is the Antichrist or simply his apostle, so greatly is the truth distorted in his decretals.

91. Luther, *Letter to Lang*, August 18, 1520. Enders, II, 461.

We are persuaded that the papacy is the seat of the Antichrist.

92. Erasmus on Luther. Erasmus, *Letter to George Spalatin*, July 6, 1520. Allen, IV, p. 298.

In Luther's opponents I see more of the spirit of this world than of the Spirit of God. I wish Luther himself would be quiet for a while. He injures learning and does himself no good, while morals and manners grow worse and worse. Truth need not always be advanced, and it makes much difference how it is proclaimed.

93. Erasmus, *Letter to Pope Leo X,* September 13, 1520. Allen, IV, 344–345.

I trust your Holiness will not listen to the calumnies against Reuchlin and me. We are charged with being in confederacy with Luther. I have always protested against this. Neither of us has anything to do with Luther. I do not know him; I have not read his writings; I have barely glanced at a few pages. . . . I supported him in so far as I thought him right, but I was the first to scent danger. I warned Froben, the printer, against printing his works. . . . I told Luther in a letter that he has friends in Louvain, but that he must moderate his style if he wished to keep them. This was two years ago, before the quarrel was so much embittered. . . . When I said I disapproved of the character of the attacks on him I was thinking less of the man himself than of the overbearing attitude of the theologians. If they had first answered and confuted him they might then have burnt his books, and himself too if he had deserved it. But the minds of a free nation cannot be driven. It would have been better for the theologians themselves if they had taken my advice and followed it.

94. Erasmus, *Letter to Aloisius Marlianus,* March 25, 1521. Allen, IV, 459–461.

You caution me against entangling myself with Luther. I have accepted your advice, and have done my utmost to keep things quiet. Luther's followers have urged me to join them, and Luther's enemies have done their best to drive me into his camp by their furious attacks on me in their sermons. Neither have succeeded. Christ I know; Luther I know not. The Roman Church I know, and death will not part me from it till the Church departs from Christ. I have always abhorred sedition, and I wish that Luther and the Germans abhorred it equally. . . . I am surprised at Aleander; we were once friends. He was instructed to conciliate, when he was sent over. He would have done better to act with me. . . . They pretend that Luther borrowed from me. No lie can be more impudent. He may have borrowed from me as heretics borrow from Evangelists and Apostles, but not a syllable else. . . . We must bear almost anything rather than throw the world into confusion. There are seasons when we must even conceal the truth. . . . They have asked me to draw up a formula of faith. I reply that I know of none save the creed of the Roman Catholic Church. . . . I feared always that revolution would be the end, and I would have done more had I not been afraid that I might be found fighting against the Spirit of God.

95. Erasmus, *Letter to Pope Adrian VI,* March 22, 1523. Allen, V, 258.

As to writing against Luther, I have not learning enough. You think my words will have authority. Alas, my popularity, such as I had, is turned into hatred. Once I was Prince of Letters, Star of Germany, Sun of Studies. . . . The note is altered now. One party says I agree with Luther because I do not oppose him. The other finds fault with me because I do oppose him. I did not anticipate what a time was coming. I admit that I helped to bring it on.

96. Adrian of Utrecht, the later Pope Adrian VI, *Letter to the Dean and the Faculty of Theology at Louvain,* December 4, 1521. Translation in P. Smith, *Letters,* I, 256.

I saw the errors which you copied from the divers writings of Luther and sent to me; they are such crude and palpable heresies on their face that even a pupil of theology in the first grade ought to have been struck by them. You certainly deserve praise for having resisted, as much as you could, the pestiferous dogmas of the man.

97. Thomas Murner, *Letter to Luther,* December, 1520. Translation in P. Smith, *Letters,* I, 431.

All Christendom, Martin Luther, would rejoice in you as a particularly learned man, if only you did not use your learning and clear reason to hurt the fatherland and destroy the faith and laws of the Fathers, and if you did not enjoy writing with a sword as much as anyone. For this cause we are obliged to defend ourselves against you as against a renegade enemy.

XI. JUSTIFICATION BY FAITH AND OTHER NEW DOCTRINES
.(1520)

98. Luther's famous treatise *On the Liberty of a Christian Man,* published in his *Works,* VII, 39–73. The title is *Epistula Lutheriana ad Leonem Decimum, Tractatus de Libertate Christiana.* It was composed in September–October, 1520. An English translation is found in H. Wace and C. A. Buchheim, *First Principles of the Reformation.* This translation was used in selecting the

following extracts. See pp. 110–111, 113, 115–117, 121, 123.

The highest worship of God is to ascribe to him truth, righteousness, and whatever qualities we must ascribe to one in whom we believe. In doing this the soul shows itself prepared to do his whole will; in doing this it hallows his name, and gives itself up to be dealt with as it may please God. For it cleaves to his promises, and never doubts that he is true, just, and wise, and will do, dispose, and provide for all things in the best way. Is not such a soul, in this its faith, most obedient to God in all things? What commandment does there remain which has not been amply fulfilled by such an obedience? What fulfillment can be more full than universal obedience? Now this is not accomplished by works, but by faith alone. . . .

On the other hand, what greater rebellion, impiety, or insult to God can there be, than not to believe his promises? What else is this, than either to make God a liar, or to doubt the truth—that is, to attribute truth to ourselves, to God falsehood and levity? In doing this, is not a man denying God and setting himself up as an idol in his own heart? What then can works, done in such a state of impiety, profit us, were they even angelic or apostolic works? . . .

If you were nothing but good works from the soles of your feet to the crown of your head, you would not be worshipping God, nor fulfilling the first commandment, since it is impossible to worship God, without ascribing to him the glory of truth and universal goodness, as it ought in truth to be ascribed. Now this is not done by works, but only by faith of heart. It is not by working, but by believing, that we glorify God, and confess him to be true. On this ground faith is the sole righteousness of a Christian man, and the fulfilling of all the commandments. For to him who fulfills the first, the task of fulfilling all the rest is easy. . . .

Nor are we only kings and the freest of all men, but also priests forever, a dignity far higher than kingship, because by that priesthood we are worthy to appear before God, to pray for others, and to teach one another mutually things which are of God. For these are the duties of the priests, and they cannot possibly be permitted to any unbeliever. . . .

Here you will ask: "If all who are in the church are priests, by what character are those, whom we now call priests, to be distinguished from the laity?" I reply: By the use of these words, "priest," "clergy," "spiritual person," "ecclesiastic," an injustice has been done, since they have been transferred from the remaining body of Christians to those few, who are now, by a hurtful custom, called ecclesiatics. For Holy Scripture makes no distinction between them, except that those, who are now boastfully called popes, bishops, and lords, it calls ministers, servants, and stewards, who are to serve the rest in the ministry of the Word, for teaching the faith of Christ and the liberty of believers. For though it is true that we are all equally priests, yet we cannot, nor, if we could, ought we all to minister and teach publicly. Thus Paul says: "Let a man so account of us as of the ministers of Christ, and stewards of the mysteries of God" (I Cor. IV). . . .

We do not then reject good works; nay, we embrace them and teach them in the highest degree. It is not on their own account that we condemn them, but on account of this impious addition to them, and the perverse notion of seeking justification by them.

99. The need of reform in doctrines, rites, and customs. Luther, *Address to the German Nobility*, composed in German. The title is *An den Christlichen Adel Deutscher Nation von des Christlichen Standes Besserung*. It was published in Luther's *Works*, VI, 404–465. See also O. Clemen, *Luthers Werke in Auswahl*, I, 363–425. An English translation is found in H. Wace and C. A. Buchheim, *First Principles of the Reformation*, pp. 17–92. The following extracts correspond to pp. 20, 31, 32, 44, 45, 46, 48, 52, 54, 56, 63, 65, 78.

I. THE THREE WALLS OF THE ROMANISTS

The Romanists have, with great adroitness, drawn three walls round themselves, with which they have hitherto protected themselves, so that no one could reform them, whereby all Christendom has fallen terribly.

Firstly, if pressed by the temporal power, they have affirmed and maintained that the temporal power has no jurisdiction over them, but on the contrary that the spiritual power is above the temporal.

Secondly, if it were proposed to admonish them with the Scriptures, they objected that no one may interpret the Scriptures but the Pope.

Thirdly, if they are threatened with a Council, they pretend that no one may call a Council but the Pope.

II. OF THE MATTERS TO BE CONSIDERED IN THE COUNCILS

1. It is a distressing and terrible thing to see that the head of Christendom, who boasts of being the Vicar of Christ and the successor of St. Peter, lives in a worldly

pomp that no king or emperor can equal: so that in him
that calls himself most holy and most spiritual, there is more
worldliness than in the world itself. He wears a triple crown,
whereas the mightiest kings only wear one crown. If this
resembles the poverty of Christ and St. Peter, it is a new
sort of resemblance. They prate of its being heretical to
object to this; nay, they will not even hear how unchristian
and ungodly it is. But I think that if he should have
to pray to God with tears, he would have to lay down
his crown; for God will not endure any arrogance. His
office should be nothing else than to weep and pray
constantly for Christendom, and to be an example of all
humility.

2. What is the use in Christendom of the people called
"Cardinals"? I will tell you. In Italy and Germany there
are many rich convents, endowments, fiefs, and benefices,
and as the best way of getting these into the hands of Rome,
they created cardinals, and gave them the sees, convents,
and prelacies, and thus destroyed the service of God. That
is why Italy is almost a desert now: the convents are destroyed, the sees consumed, the revenues of the prelacies
and of all the churches drawn to Rome; towns are decayed;
the country and people ruined, while there is no more any
worship of God or preaching; why? Because the cardinals
must have all the wealth. No Turk could have thus deso-
lated Italy and overthrown the worship of God.

III. TWENTY-SEVEN ARTICLES RESPECTING THE
REFORMATION OF THE CHRISTIAN ESTATE

Now though I am too lowly to submit articles that could
serve for the reformation of these fearful evils, I will yet
sing out my fool's song, and will show, as well as my wit

will allow, what might and should be done by the temporal authorities or by a General Council.

3. It should be decreed by an Imperial law, that no episcopal cloak, and no confirmation of any appointment shall for the future be obtained from Rome.

4. Let it be decreed that no temporal matter shall be submitted to Rome, but all shall be left to the jurisdiction of the temporal authorities.

5. Henceforth no reservations shall be valid, and no benefices shall be appropriated by Rome, whether the incumbent die, or there be a dispute, or the incumbent be a servant of the Pope, or of a Cardinal.

10. The Pope must withdraw his hand from the dish, and on no pretence assume royal authority over Naples and Sicily. He has no more right to it than I, and yet claims to be the lord of it.

12. Pilgrimages to Rome must be abolished, or at least no one must be allowed to go from his own wish or his own piety, unless his priest, his town magistrate, or his lord has found that there is sufficient reason for his pilgrimage.

13. Now we come to the great crowd that promises much and performs little. Be not angry, my good sirs, I mean well. I have to tell you this bitter and sweet truth! Let no more mendicant monasteries be built! God help us! There are too many as it is. Would to God they were all abolished, or at least made over to two or three orders. It has never done good, it will never do good, to go wandering about over the country. Therefore my advice is that ten, or as many as required, may be put together and made into one, which one, sufficiently provided for, is not to beg.

16. It were also right to abolish annual festivals, processions, and masses for the dead, or at least to diminish

their number; for we evidently see that they have become no better than a mockery, exciting the anger of God, and having no object but money-getting, eating, and drinking.

18. One should abolish all saints' days, keeping only Sunday.

25. The universities also require a good, sound Reformation. I must say this, let it vex whom it may. The fact is that whatever the Papacy has ordered or instituted is only designed for the propagation of sin and error. What are the universities, as at present ordered, but as the Book of Maccabees says: "Schools of 'Greek fashion' and heathenish manners" (II Maccab. IV, 12–13); full of dissolute living where very little is taught of the Holy Scriptures and of the Christian faith, and the blind heathen teacher, Aristotle, rules even further than Christ? Now, my advice would be that the books of Aristotle, the *Physics,* the *Metaphysics, Of the Soul, Ethics,* which have hitherto been considered the best, be altogether abolished, with all others that profess to treat of nature, though nothing can be learned from them, either of natural or of spiritual things.

100. On the Sacraments. Luther, *On the Babylonish Captivity of the Church.* Written in Latin and entitled *De Captivate Babylonica Ecclesiae Praeludium.* Published in Luther's *Works,* Weimar edition, VI, 497–573. See also O. Clemen, *Luthers Werke in Auswahl,* I, 426–512. Buchheim, *First Principles of the Reformation,* pp. 141–246. The following extracts correspond to pp. 141–142, 147, 149, 155–156, 158, 176, 177, 190, 193, 197–198, 200–201, 205–206, 209–211, 214, 215–216, 224, 227–228, 237–238.

Whether I will or not, I am compelled to become more learned day by day, since so many great masters vie with each other in urging me on and giving me practice. I wrote about indulgences two years ago, but now I extremely regret having published the book. At that time I was still involved in a great and superstitious respect for the tyranny of Rome, which led me to judge that indulgences were not to be totally rejected, seeing them, as I did, to be approved by so general a consent among men. And no wonder, for at that time it was I alone who was rolling this stone. Afterwards, however, with the kind aid of Sylvester, and the friars, who supported indulgences so strenuously, I perceived that they were nothing but mere impostures of the flatterers of Rome, whereby to make away with the faith of God and the money of men. And I wish I could prevail upon the booksellers, and persuade all who have read them, to burn the whole of my writings on indulgences, and in place of all I have written about them to adopt this proposition: Indulgences are wicked devices of the flatterers of Rome. . . .

After this, Eccius and Emser, with their fellow-conspirators, began to instruct me concerning the primacy of the Pope. Here too, not to be ungrateful to such learned men, I must confess that their works helped me on greatly; for, while I had denied that the Papacy had any divine right, I still admitted that it had a human right. But after hearing and reading the supersubtle subtleties of those coxcombs, by which they so ingeniously set up their idol—my mind being not entirely unteachable in such matters—I now know and am sure that the Papacy is the kingdom of Babylon, and the power of Nimrod the mighty hunter. Here, moreover, that all may go prosperously with my friends, I entreat the booksellers, and entreat my readers, to burn all that I have published on this subject, and to hold to the fol-

lowing proposition: The Papacy is the mighty hunting of
the Bishop of Rome. . . .

To begin I must deny that there are seven Sacraments,
and must lay it down, for the time being, that there are only
three, baptism, penance, and the communion, and that by
the Court of Rome all these have been brought into miserable bondage, and the Church despoiled of all her liberty.
And yet, if I were to speak according to the usage of Scripture, I should hold that there was only one sacrament, and
three sacramental signs.

Concerning the Lord's Supper

But suppose me to be standing on the other side and ques-
tioning my lords the papists. In the Supper of the Lord, the
whole sacrament, or the sacrament in both kinds, was either
given to the presbyters alone (for thus they will have it to
be), then it is in no wise lawful that any kind should be
given to the laity; for it ought not to be rashly given to any,
to whom Christ did not give it at the first institution. Otherwise, if we allow one of Christ's institutions to be
changed, we make the whole body of His laws of no effect;
and any man may venture to say that he is bound by no law
or institution of Christ. For in dealing with Scripture one
special exception does away with any general statement.
If, on the other hand, it was given to the laity as well, it
even inevitably follows that reception in both kinds ought
not to be denied to the laity; and in denying it to them
when they seek it, we act impiously, and contrary to the
deed, example, and institution of Christ. . . .

Formerly, when I was imbibing the scholastic theology,
my lord the Cardinal of Cambray gave me occasion for

reflection, by arguing most acutely, in the fourth book of the *Sentences,* that it would be much more probable, and that fewer superfluous miracles would have to be introduced, if real bread and real wine, and not only their accidents, were understood to be upon the altar, unless the church had determined the contrary. Afterwards, when I saw what church it was, which had thus determined, namely, the Thomistic, that is, the Aristotelian Church, I became bolder, and whereas I had been before in great straits of doubt, I now at length established my conscience in the former opinion, namely, that there were real bread and real wine, in which were the real flesh and the real blood of Christ, in no other manner and in no less degree than the other party assert them to be under the accidents. And this I did, because I saw that the opinions of the Thomists, whether approved by the Pope or by a council, remained opinions, and did not become articles of faith, even were an angel from heaven to decree otherwise. For that which is asserted without the support of the Scriptures, or of an approved revelation, it is permitted to hold as an opinion, but it is not necessary to believe. . . .

But why should not Christ be able to include His body within the substance of bread, as well as within the accidents? Fire and iron, two different substances, are so mingled in red hot iron, that every part of it is both fire and iron. Why may not the glorious body of Christ much more be in every part of the substance of bread?

We must also get rid of another scandal, which is a much greater and a very specious one; that is, that the mass is universally believed to be a sacrifice offered to God. With this opinion the words of the canon of the mass appear to agree, such as—"These gifts; these offerings; these holy sacrifices;" and again, "this oblation." There is also a very distinct prayer that the sacrifice may be accepted like the sacrifice of Abel; hence Christ is called the victim of the altar. To this we must add the sayings of the Holy Fathers, a great number of authorities, and the usage that has been constantly observed throughout the world. . . .

To all these difficulties, which beset us so pertinaciously, we must oppose with the utmost constancy the words and example of Christ. Unless we hold the mass to be the promise or testament of Christ, according to the plain meaning of the words, we lose all the gospel and our whole comfort. So let us allow nothing to prevail against these words; even if an angel from heaven taught us otherwise. Now in these words there is nothing about a work or sacrifice. Again, we have the example of Christ on our side. When Christ instituted this sacrament and established this testament in the Last Supper, he did not offer himself to God the Father or accomplish any work on behalf of others, but, as he sat at the table, he declared the same testament to each individual present and bestowed on each the sign of it. Now the more any mass resembles and is akin to that first mass of all which Christ celebrated at the Last Supper, the more Christian it is. But that mass of Christ was most simple; without any display of vestments, gestures, hymns, and other ceremonies; so that if it had been necessary that it should be offered as a sacrifice, his institution of it would not have been complete.

Concerning the Sacrament of Baptism

Thus it is not baptism which justifies any man, or is of any advantage; but faith in that word of promise to which baptism is added, for this justifies and fulfills the meaning of baptism. For faith is the submerging of the old man, and the emerging of the new man. Hence it cannot be that the new sacraments differ from the ancient sacraments, for they both alike have divine promises and the same spirit of faith; but they differ incomparably from the ancient figures, on account of the word of promise, which is the sole and most effective means of difference. . . .

We must therefore keep clear of the error of those who have reduced the effect of baptism to such small and slender dimensions that, while they say that grace is infused by it, they assert that this grace is afterwards, so to speak, effused by sin; and that we must then go to heaven by some other way, as if baptism had now become absolutely useless. Do not thou judge thus, but understand that the significance of baptism is such that thou mayest live and die in it; and that neither by penitence nor by any other way canst do ought but return to the effect of baptism, and do afresh what thou wert baptized in order to do, and what thy baptism signified.

In opposition to what I have said, an argument will perhaps be drawn from the baptism of infants, who cannot receive the promise of God, or have faith in their baptism; and it will be said that therefore either faith is not requisite, or infants are baptized in vain. To this I reply, what all men say, that infants are aided by faith of others, namely, that of those who bring them to baptism. For as the word of God, when it is preached, is powerful enough to change the heart of a wicked man, which is not less devoid of sense and feeling than any infant, so through the prayers of the Church, which bring the child in faith, to which prayers all things are possible, the infant is changed, cleansed, and renewed by faith infused into it. Nor should I doubt that even a wicked adult, if the Church were to bring him forward and pray for him, might undergo a change in any of the sacraments; just as we read in the gospel that the paralytic man was healed by the faith of others. . . .

I should certainly not forbid or object to any vow which a man may make of his own private choice. I do not wish altogether to condemn or depreciate vows; but my advice would be altogether against the public establishment or confirmation of any such mode of life. It is enough that every man should be at liberty to make private vows at his own peril; but that a public system of living under the constraint of vows should be inculcated, I consider to be a thing pernicious to the Church and to all simple souls. In the first place, it is not a little repugnant to the Christian life, inasmuch as a vow is a kind of ceremonial law, and a matter of human tradition or invention; from all which the Church has been set free by baptism, since the Christian is bound by no law, except that of God. Moreover, there is no example of it in the Scriptures, especially of the vow of perpetual chastity, obedience, and poverty. Now a vow of which we have no example in the Scriptures is a perilous one, which ought to be urged upon no man, much less be established as a common and public mode of life; even if every individual must be allowed to venture upon it at his own peril, if he will. There are some works which are wrought by the Spirit in but few, and these ought by no means to be brought forward as an example, or as a manner of life. . . .

I greatly fear, however, that these systems of living under vows in the religious, are of the number of those things of which the Apostle foretold: "Speaking lies in hypocrisy; forbidding to marry, and commanding to abstain from meats, which God hath created to be received with thanksgiving" (I Tim. IV, 2-3). Let no one cite against me the example of St. Bernard, St. Francis, St. Dominic, and such like authors or supporters of religious orders. God is terrible and wonderful in his dealings with the children of men. He may have sanctified the men of whom I have spoken in their perilous mode of life, and have guided them by the special working of his Spirit; while yet he would not have this mode an example for other men. It is certain that not one of these men was saved by his vows or his religious order, but by faith alone, by which all men are saved, but to which these showy servitudes of vows are especially hostile.

Concerning the Sacrament of Penance

In this third part I shall speak of the sacrament of penance. By the tracts and disputations which I have published on this subject I have given offence to very many; and have amply expressed my own opinions. I must now briefly repeat these statements, in order to unveil the tyranny which attacks us on this point as unsparingly as in the sacrament of the bread. In these two sacraments gain and lucre find a place, and therefore the avarice of the shepherds has raged to an incredible extent against the sheep of Christ; while even baptism, as we have seen in speaking of vows, has been sadly obscured among adults, that the purposes of avarice might be served. . . .

The first and capital evil connected with this sacrament is, that they have totally done away with the sacrament itself, leaving not even a vestige of it. Whereas this, like the other sacraments, consists of the word of the divine promise on one side and of our faith on the other; they have overthrown both of these. They have adopted to the purposes of their own tyranny Christ's word of promise when He says: "Whatsoever thou shalt bind on earth shall be bound in heaven: and whatsoever thou shall loose on earth shall be loosed in heaven" (Matt. XVI, 19); and: "Whatsoever ye shall bind on earth shall be bound in heaven; and whatsoever ye shall loose on earth shall be loosed in heaven" (Matt. XVIII, 18); and again: "Whatsoever sins ye remit, they are remitted unto them; and whosoever sins ye retain, they are retained" (John XX, 23). These words are meant to call forth the faith of the penitents, that they may seek and obtain remission of their sins. But these men, in all their books, writings, and discourses, have not made it their object to explain to Christians the promise conveyed in these words, and to show them what they ought to believe, and how much consolation they might have, but to establish in the utmost length, breadth, and depth their own powerful and violent tyranny. At last some have even begun to give orders to the angels in heaven, and to boast, with an incredible frenzy of piety, that they have received the right to rule in heaven and on earth, and have the power of binding even in heaven. Thus they say not a word about the saving faith of the people, but talk largely of the tyrannical power of the pontiffs; whereas Christ's words do not deal at all with power, but entirely with faith. . . .

There is no doubt that confession of sins is necessary, and is commanded by God. "They were baptized of John in Jordan, confessing their sins" (Matt. III, 6). "If we confess our sins, he is faithful and just to forgive us our sins. If we say that we have not sinned, we make him a liar, and his word is not in us" (I John I, 9–10). If the saints must not deny their sin, how much more ought those who are guilty of great or public offence to confess them. But the most effective proof of the institution of confession is given when Christ tells us that an offending brother must be told of his fault, brought before the Church, accused, and finally, if he neglect to hear the Church, excommunicated. He "hears" when he yields to reproof, and acknowledges and confesses his sin. . . .

The secret confession, however, which is now practised, though it cannot be proven from Scripture, is in my opinion highly satisfactory, and useful or even necessary. I could not wish it not to exist; nay, I rejoice that it does exist in the Church of Christ, for it is the one great remedy for afflicted consciences; when, after laying open our conscience to a brother, and unveiling all the evil which lay hid there, we receive direct from the mouth of that brother the word of consolation sent forth from God, receiving which by faith we find peace in a sense of the mercy of God, who speaks to us through our brother. What I protest against is the conversion of this institution of confession into a means of tyranny and extortion by the bishops. They reserve certain cases to themselves as secret, and then order them to be revealed to confessors named by themselves, and thus vex the consciences of men; filling the office of bishop, but utterly neglecting the real duties of a bishop, which are to preach the gospel and to minister to the poor. Nay, these impious tyrants principally reserve to themselves the cases which are of less consequence, while they leave the greater ones everywhere to the common herd of priests, cases such as the ridiculous inventions of the bull "In Coena Domini." . . .

From all this I do not hesitate to say that whosoever voluntarily confesses his sins privately, in the presence of any brother, or, when told of his faults, asks pardon and amends his life, is absolved from his secret sins, since Christ has manifestly bestowed the power of absolution on every believer in him, with whatever violence the pontiffs may rage against this truth.

Of Confirmation

It is surprising that it should have entered anyone's mind to make a Sacrament of Confirmation out of that laying on of hands which Christ applied to little children, and by which the apostles bestowed the Holy Spirit, ordained presbyters, and healed the sick; as the Apostle writes to Timothy: "Lay hands suddenly on no man" (I Tim. V, 22). . . .

I do not say this because I condemn the seven sacraments, but because I deny that they can be proved from the Scriptures. I wish there were in the Church such a laying on of hands as there was in the time of the Apostles, whether we chose to call it confirmation or healing. As it is, however, none of it remains, except so much as we have ourselves invented in order to regulate the duties of the bishops, that they may not be entirely without work in the church.

Of Matrimony

It is not only without any warrant of Scripture that matrimony is considered a sacrament, but it has been turned into a mere mockery by the very same traditions which vaunt it as a sacrament. Let us look a little into this. I have said that in every sacrament there is contained a word of divine promise, which must be believed in by him who receives the sign; and that the sign alone cannot constitute a sacrament. Now we nowhere read that he who marries a wife will receive any grace from God; neither is there in matrimony any sign of divine institution, nor do we anywhere read that it was appointed of God to be a sign of anything; although it is true that all visible transactions may be understood as figures and allegorical representations of visible things. But figures and allegories are not sacraments, in the sense in which we are speaking of sacraments. . . .

Furthermore, since matrimony has existed since the beginning of the world, and still continues even among unbelievers, there are no reasons why it should be called a sacrament of the new law, and of the Church alone. . . .

The impediment of holy orders is also a mere contrivance of man, especially when they idly assert that even a marriage already contracted is annulled by this cause, always exalting their own traditions above the commands of God. I give no judgment respecting the order of priesthood, such as it is at the present day; but I see that Paul commands that a bishop should be the husband of one wife, and therefore the marriage of a deacon, of a priest, of a bishop, or of a man in any kind of orders, cannot be annulled; although Paul knew nothing of that kind of priests and those orders which we have at the present day.

Of Orders

Of this sacrament, the Church of Christ knows nothing; it was invented by the Church of the Pope. It not only has no promise of grace, anywhere declared, but not a word is said about it in the whole of the New Testament. Now it is ridiculous to set up as a sacrament of God that which can nowhere be proved to have been instituted by God. Not that I consider that a rite practised for so many ages is to be condemned; but I would not have human inventions established in sacred things, nor should it be allowed to bring in anything as divinely ordained, which has not been divinely ordained; which has not been ever ordained, lest we should be objects of ridicule to our adversaries. . . .

See then how far the glory of the Church has departed. The whole world is full of priests, bishops, cardinals, and clergy; of whom, however (so far as concerns their official duty), not one preaches—unless he be called afresh to this by another calling besides his sacramental orders—but thinks that he amply fulfills the purposes of that sacrament if he murmurs over in a vain repetition, the prayers which he has to read, and celebrates masses. Even then, he never prays these very hours, or, if he does pray, he prays for himself; while, as the very height of perversity, he offers up his masses as a sacrifice, though the mass is really the use of the sacrament. Thus it is clear that those orders by which, as a sacrament, men of this kind are ordained to be clergy, are in truth a mere and entire figment, invented by men who understand nothing of church affairs, of the priesthood, of the ministry of the word, or of the sacraments. Such as is the sacrament, such are the priests it makes.

On the Sacrament of Extreme Unction

To this rite of anointing the sick our theologians have made two additions well worthy of themselves. One is, that they call it a sacrament; the other, that they make it extreme, so that it cannot be administered except to those who are in extreme peril of life. Perhaps—as they are keen dialecticians—they have so made it in relation to the first unction of baptism, and the two following ones of confirmation and orders. They have this, it is true, to throw in my teeth, that, on the authority of the Apostle James, there are in this case, a promise and a sign, which two things, I have

hitherto said, constitute a sacrament. He says: "Is any sick
among you? let him call for the elders of the church, and
let them pray over him, anointing him with oil in the name
of the Lord; and the prayer of faith shall save the sick, and
the Lord shall raise him up; and if he have committed
sins, they shall be forgiven him" (James V, 14–15). Here,
they say, is the promise of remission of sins, and the sign
of the oil. . . .

I, however, say that if folly has ever been uttered, it has
been uttered on this subject. I pass over the fact that many
assert, and with great probability, that this epistle was not
written by the Apostle James, and is not worthy of the apostolic spirit; although, whosoever it is, it has obtained authority by usage. Still, even if it were written by the Apostle
James, I should say that it was not lawful for an apostle
to institute a sacrament by his own authority; that is, to
give a divine promise with a sign annexed to it. To do
this belonged to Christ alone.

XII. STORM AND STRESS (1521–1522)

101. The Papal Bull "Exurge Domine," June 15, 1520.
Printed at Rome, 1520. Reprinted in B. J. Kidd, *Documents of the Continental Reformation*, no. 38.

Forty-one Propositions drawn from Luther's work are
hereby condemned as heretical, scandalous, offensive to pious
ears, insulting, ensnaring, and contrary to Catholic truth.

102. Luther, *Letter to Spalatin*, December 10, 1520. Enders, III, 18.

In the year 1520, on December 10, at nine o'clock, at the
eastern gate, near the Church of the Holy Cross, were

burned all the papal books, the *Decretum,* the *Decretals,* *Liber Sextus,* the *Clementines,* the *Extravagantes,* and the latest bull of Leo X.

103. Luther before the Diet at Worms, April 18, 1521. *Reichstagsakten,* new series, 1896, ed. A. Wrede, vol. II, section VII. J. Kidd, *Documents,* no. 42.

Your Majesty the Emperor and you illustrious princes asked me two questions yesterday; namely, whether these books which bear my name I acknowledge as mine, and whether I will retract the doctrines I have propounded therein. Yesterday I gave a prompt and plain answer to the first question, saying that these books are mine. I shall persist in this reply until the end of my life, provided that malice, trickery, or unseasonable prudence do not effect any alteration in them. Before I reply to the second question, I entreat your Majesty and Lordships to consider that my books do not all treat of the same matter. There are some in which I have discussed simply and in accordance with the Gospel the advancement of piety and faith and the improvement of morals, so that even my adversaries admit that these books are harmless and worthy of Christian reading. If I were to disown them, what should I be doing? I should be the only one among all mortals to condemn a truth which friends and enemies alike confess. There is another sort of writings, in which I have attacked the papacy and the opinions of the papists as the destruction of sound doctrines and the damnation of soul and body. If I were to deny these writings, I should lend fresh force and audacity to the tyranny of Rome. My recantation would only serve to extend the kingdom of iniquity; especially when it should be known that it was by orders of his Majesty and of the whole Roman Empire. Finally, there are my polemical writings, directed to some of my adversaries, supporters of the tyranny of Rome. I shall readily admit that I have shown myself more violent in them than is becoming a man of my calling. I do not act the saint here, I do not dispute upon my own conduct, but rather upon Christ's doctrines. I cannot, moreover, consent to disavow these writings, because Rome would avail itself of my admission to extend her kingdom and oppress souls. Being a man, and not God, I cannot protect my books with any other patronage than that with which Christ protected his doctrines. When questioned before Annas as to what he taught, he said, "If I have spoken evil, show me how."

Since, then, your Majesty and Lordships demand a simply response, I will give it. Unless convinced by proofs from Scripture or by clear reasons—for I believe neither Pope nor councils alone, since it is certain they have often erred and contradicted themselves—I cannot and will not revoke anything.

104. Luther claims to have created no new theology. Luther, *Eine treue Vermahnung zu allen Christen, sich zu hüten vor Aufruhr und Empörung.* December, 1521. Printed in Luther's *Werke,* Weimar edition, VIII, 676–687; O. Clemen, *Auswahl,* II, 300–310. The following extract is from p. 685 (308).

I beg that my name be passed over in silence, and that people call themselves not Lutheran, but Christian. What is Luther? My teaching is not mine. Saint Paul did not want Christians to be called Paulinians, but Christians. (I Cor. III.)

105. Luther, *Letter to Nicholas Gerbel of Strassburg,* November 1, 1521. Enders, III, 240.

Believe me, I am exposed in this quiet hermitage to a thousand devils. It is far more easy to fight against men, who are devils incarnate, than against the "spirits of wickedness, dwelling in high places" (Ephes. VI, 12). I fall often, but the right hand of the Lord raises me up again.

106. Luther, *Letter to Spalatin,* August 15, 1521. Enders, III, 219.

I would gladly see celibacy made optional, as the Gospel wills, but I do not yet see how I can prove it.

107. Luther, *Letter to Melanchthon,* September 9, 1521. Enders, III, 224.

Whoever has taken a vow in a spirit opposed to evangelical freedom must be set free.

108. Luther translates the Bible. Luther, *Letter to Spalatin,* March 30, 1522. Enders.

I have not only translated the Gospel of John, but the whole of the New Testament, and Philip and I are now busy correcting it. This book is to be written in the simplest language, that all may understand it.

109. Luther, *Preface to the Exposition of I Peter,* 1523. B. J. Kidd, *Documents,* no. 55.

Those apostles who treat most frequently and excellently of how faith in Christ alone justifies, are the best Evangelists. Therefore, the Epistles of Paul are more of a Gospel than Matthew, Mark, and Luke.

110. Luther, *Preface to the New Testament*, 1524. Same source as above.

John's Gospel, Paul's Epistles, especially that to the Romans, and Peter's First Epistle are the right kernel and marrow of all books, for in them you find written down not many works and miracles of Christ, but in quite a masterly way the exposition of how faith in Christ overcomes sin and death, and gives life, righteousness, and peace. Therefore the Epistle of James in comparison with these is a mere letter of straw.

111. Luther condemns the radicals who during his stay in the Wartburg Castle (April, 1521–March 1, 1522) caused dissension in Wittenberg. Luther, *Letter to Spalatin*, January 17, 1522. Enders, III.

Rumors are circulated to the effect that changes have been made in the sacrament of the Lord's Supper. I went to Wittenberg before, but now I daily hear of greater changes.

112. Luther, *Letter to Wenceslaus Link*, March 19, 1522. Enders, III, 1522.

Satan invaded my sheepfold and caused the liberty of the spirit to be changed into the license of the flesh, and when the service of love had been lost, to confound everything by a dreadful scism. Carlstadt and Gabriel Zwilling were the originators of these monstrosities. This was the reason why I returned, so that I might, if Christ were willing, destroy this work of Satan.

113. Luther, *Letter to Spalatin,* March 12, 1522. Erlangen edition, LIII, 114.

Let Carlstadt persist or not, Christ will know how to bring his wicked efforts to an end.

114. King Henry VIII of England attacks Luther in his *Assertio Septem Sacramentorum adversus Martinum Lutherum,* or *Defense of the Seven Sacraments against Martin Luther.* The first edition of this book appeared in 1521, published by Pynson at London. Two new editions were printed at Antwerp in 1522. The following quotation is from the Paris edition of 1652, p. 10.

There was a time when the faith had no need of defenders; it had no enemies. Now it has one who exceeds in malignity all his predecessors, who is instigated by the devil, who covers himself with the shield of charity, and, full of hatred and wrath, discharges his viperish venom against the Church and Catholicism. . . . What similar pestilence has ever attacked the Lord's flock? What serpent can be compared with this monk who has written upon the Babylonish captivity of the Church? . . . To this scoffer of our old traditions, who puts no faith in our holy fathers, or the ancient interpreters of our holy books, except when they agree with him; who compares the Holy See to the impure Babylon, treats as a tyrant the sovereign pontiff, and makes that holy name synonymous with Antichrist?

115. Luther, *Contra Henricum Regem Angliae,* in his *Works,* Weimar edition, X, 227–234 (German version).

It is two years since I published a small book, entitled *The Captivity of the Church in Babylon*. It has annoyed the Papists, who have spared neither falsehoods nor abuse against me. I willingly forgive them. . . . The Lord Henry, not by the grace of God, king of England, has recently written in Latin against that treatise. . . . If a king of England spits his impudent lies in my face, I am entitled on my part to thrust them down his throat. . . . What astonishes me, is not the ignorance of King Henry—not that he understands less of faith and works than a block does about God; it is that the devil thus plays the clown by means of his Henry, although he knows well that I laugh at him.

XIII. LUTHER'S MARRIAGE (1525)

116. (Matrimony recommended.) Luther, *Letter to W. Reissenbusch,* March 27, 1525. Enders, V, 145. See Erlangen edition for the complete text, vol. LIII, 286.

Whoever wishes to remain single, let him put away his human name and fashion himself into an angel or a spirit, for to a man does God not give this grace.

117. Luther marries Catherine von Bora. Luther, *Letter to L. Koppe of Torgau,* June 17, 1525. Erlangen edition, LIII, 321.

Most worthy Father Prior, you know what has happened to me, namely that the nun whom two years ago you carried off from the convent is nevertheless returning to the cloister; not this time, however, to take the veil, but as the honored wife of Dr. Luther, who up till now has lived in the old empty Augustinian Monastery in Wittenberg.

118. Luther, *Letter to John Rühel, J. Thür, and C. Müller,* June 15, 1525. Enders, V, 195; Erlangen edition, LIII, 314.

Thus, so far as I am able, I have by marriage thrown away the last remnant of my former papish life.

XIV. THE PEASANTS' WAR (1525)

119. Luther attacks the nobles, and reprimands the peasants. Luther, *Ermahnung zum Frieden auf de Zwölf Artickel der Bauernschaft in Schwaben.* Composed April–May, 1525. Printed in Luther's *Works,* XVIII, 291–345; O. Clemen, *Auswahl,* III, 47–93. The following extracts are from pp. 293, 299–300.

On you first, princes and lords, devolves the responsibility for these tumults and seditions; on you especially, blind bishops, stupid priests, and monks. You, who persist in playing the fool and attacking the Gospel, know perfectly well that it will stand firm against your assaults. . . .

My brethren, the peasants, the princes who oppose the propagation of the Gospel light among you are deserving of God's vengeance; they merit dethronement. But would you not be also guilty, were you to stain your hands and souls with the blood which you intend to shed? You have taken up the sword,—you shall perish by the sword. In resisting your rulers, you resist Jesus Christ. You ask to be permitted to hear the Gospel in liberty. Can't you change your residence and come here to drink at the source of the Divine Word?

120. Luther advises that the rebellious peasants be killed.
   Luther, *Ein Sendbrief von dem harten Büchlein wider
   die Bauern,* July, 1525. Luther's *Works,* XVIII, 384–
   401; O. Clemen, *Auswahl,* III, 75–93.

As I wrote in my treatise against the peasants, so I write
now. Let no one take pity on the hardened, obstinate, and
blinded peasants who will not listen; let anyone who can
and is able, hew down, stab and slay them as one would a
mad dog. An ass must be beaten and the rabble governed by
force. The intention of the devil was to lay Germany waste,
because he was unable to prevent in any other way the
spread of the Gospel.

XV. Luther Defends his View on Predestination and Free Will (1525)

121. Luther's treatise *On the Bondage of the Will,* September–October, 1525. The title is *De Servo Arbitrio,*
   published in Luther's *Works,* XVIII, 600–787; O.
   Clemen, *Auswahl,* III, 94–293. Luther wrote it in answer to the *Diatribe on Free Will,* published by Erasmus
   in 1524. The following extract is from p. 783 (288–
   289).

As for myself, I confess that were I offered free will, I
would not have it, or any other instrument that might aid in
my salvation; not only because, besieged by so many perils
and adversities, amidst that horde of devils who assail me
on all sides, it would be impossible for me to preserve or
make use of that instrument of salvation, since one devil is
stronger than all men put together, and no way of real
salvation would be open to me; but because, were the

dangers surmounted, and the devils put to flight, I should labor in uncertainty, and my aim would be fatigued to no purpose by beating the air with useless blows. For, were I to live forever, my conscience would never be certain of having satisfied God. . . .

But since God has taken charge of my salvation, independently of my free will, and has promised to save me by his grace and his mercy without the concurrence of my works, I am certain that he will be faithful to his promise, that he will not lie, and that he is powerful enough to prevent me from being broken by adversity or carried off by the devil. So then, if all are not elect, much fewer will be so, while by free will none could be saved, and all would perish.

XVI. The Formation of a New Church
(1525–1530)

122. Church visitation. Luther, *Letter to the Elector John,* November 30, 1525. Erlangen edition, LIII, 336.

I suggest that you should order all the churches in your dominions to be visited, and where the people desire Evangelical preachers, and the funds are inadequate for their maintenance, let them receive so much yearly, either from the town council or elsewhere.

123. Luther, *Letter to the Elector John of Saxony,* November 22, 1526. Erlangen edition, LIII, 386.

The farmer will give nothing, and there is so much ingratitude among the people for the Word of God that he will no doubt send a plague among us. We are commanded to look after the poor children, and train them in the nurture and admonition of the Lord. We think it necessary that four persons visit all the country and see to the maintenance of schools and Church livings.

124. The Order of Worship. Luther, *Deutsche Messe*, January, 1526. Luther's *Works*, Weimar ed., XIX, 72–113; O. Clemen, *Auswahl*, III, 294–309.

Before all things I beg those who examine this order of worship and desire to follow it, not to make out of it a binding rule or restrain any one's conscience, but to use it in accordance with Christian liberty whenever and whereever they please. . . .

In the first place a simple Catechism is necessary. A catechism is a course of instruction whereby heathens who wish to become Christians are taught what they shall believe, do, forego, and know. . . .

On Feast Days and Sundays there will be three sermons. Around five or six o'clock the people will sing some psalms; after that there will be a sermon on one of the Epistles. At eight or nine a communion service, and a sermon on one of the Gospels. In the afternoon a sermon on the Old Testament.

125. The Small Catechism. B. J. Kidd, *Documents Illustrative of the Continental Reformation*, no. 97. Dated 1529.

Though we cannot and may not force any to believe, yet we must train and urge the multitude so that they may know what is right and wrong among those with whom they live. . . .

Because the tyranny of the Pope is past, they will no longer come to the Sacrament, and despise it. We ought to preach to them, saying, "Whoever does not seek or desire the Sacrament, or demand it, at least once or four times a year, it is to be feared that he despises the Sacrament and is no Christian." If they do not come, let them go their way, and tell them that they belong to the devil. Our office has now become a real and saving office.

    I. The Ten Commandments.
   II. The Apostles' Creed.
  III. The Lord's Prayer.
  IV. The Sacrament of Holy Baptism.
   V. How the Simple Folks Should Be Taught to Confess.
  VI. The Sacrament of the Altar.

XVII. LUTHER AND ZWINGLI (1525–1530)

126. Luther, *Letter to Amsdorf*, December 2, 1524. Enders. V, 52.

Carlstadt's prison crawls far. Zwingli in Zürich has become converted to his view. And there are many others who allege that in the Sacrament there is nothing but bread, just as on the market stands.

127. Luther, *Letter to Spalatin*, January 13, 1525. Enders, V, 103.

Oecolampadius supports Carlstadt. Behold the machinations of Satan.

128. Luther, *Letter to Wenceslaus Link in Nuremberg*, May, 1527. Enders, VI, 46.

Zwingli fumes, rages, threatens, and blusters so that he appears to me hopeless.

129. Luther, *Letter to Spalatin*, June 12, 1527. Enders, VI, 62.

Bucer wrote a venomous letter against me. Luther seems to these people a veritable Satan.

130. Luther writes a Sermon on the Eucharist against the Sacramentarians, entitled *Sermon von dem Sacrament des Leibs und Bluts Christi*, 1526. In Luther's *Works*, Weimar ed., XIX, 474.

One should distinguish two factors in the Sacrament; in the first place, what one is to believe, and in the second place, how one is to partake of the Sacrament. Thus far' I have said little about the first point. But since many preachers have begun to express different opinions about the first, it is time that I enlarge on it. . . .
We have before us the plain words of Christ: "Take, eat, this is my body which is broken for you." These words are simple, so that our opponents must grant how difficult it is to get a different interpretation. If these words are not clear, I like to know how one is to speak German.

131. Melanchthon reports that Luther remains firm. Melanchthon, *Letter to Justus Jonas*, December 16, 1527. *Corpus Reformatorum*, I, no. 484 (column 914).

After we had discussed the Eucharist at great length, Luther told me what I gladly heard, that he held fast to what he had taught before.

132. Luther's principal work on the Holy Supper, entitled
Bekenntnis vom Abendmahl Christi, 1528. In Luther's
Works, XXVI, 261–509.

I am not going to write any more to Zwingli and his
friends, lest Satan get still more mad and spit out more
lies than before, and so soil the paper (p. 302).

The devil must be their teacher, for they do not agree
on the text (p. 265).

One should avoid Zwingli and his books as devilish
poison of Satan (p. 317).

Zwingli is to be avoided as a real heretic, who rejects
an article of faith. Not only does Zwingli reject this highest, most necessary article, that God's son died for us, but
blasphemes besides, saying that it is the most hideous heresy
that ever was. I confess that I consider Zwingli not a
Christian, for he does not hold any article of the Christian faith rightly; and he has become seven times worse
than he was as a papist (p. 342).

It is pure nonsense to say that the word "Is" amounts to
the same as the word "signifies." They are not able, like
children in school, to understand what "Tropus" means!
In the *Tropus* a certain word gets a new meaning. For in-
stance, when I say, "Christ is a flower," then Christ is a
real flower; not a real flower in the ground, but another.
The Scriptures are full of metaphors (p. 271).

I taught before and still teach that the flesh of Christ
is of no value, but on the contrary, it is poison and death,
when eaten without faith (p. 353).

133. Christ is present in the Eucharist. Same source as
above, pp. 414–415, 421.

Christ is simultaneously in heaven and in the Eucharist. It is as with the sun shining on the sea or a lake. Every spectator sees it from his place. When one moves his position, the reflexion of the sun moves also. . . .

If Christ is a person both divine and human, then his human nature must be present both in heaven and upon earth.

134. The Marburg debate, October 1-4, 1529. Luther, *Letter to John Agricola.* Oct. 12, 1529. Enders, VII, 169.

I replied to both Oecolampadius and Zwingli, insisting on the words, "This is my body."

135. The controversy continues. Luther, *Letter to Jacob Prost of Bremen,* June 1, 1530. Enders, VII, 353–354.

The sacramentarians are not only liars, but falsehood, deceit, and hypocrisy incarnate, as Carlstadt and Zwingli show in both deeds and words. We revoked nothing.

XVIII. The Confession of Augsburg (1530)

136. Luther remains in the Castle of Coburg. Luther, *Letter to Eoban Hesse,* April 23, 1530. Enders, VII, p. 300.

I am sending you four letters, my dear Eoban, and they are living, talking letters, namely, Justus, Philip, Spalatin, and Agricola. I should gladly have been the fifth.

137. Melanchthon presents the *Confession* at the Diet of Augsburg, June 25, 1530. Melanchthon, *Letter to*

Luther, June 25, 1530. Printed in *Corpus Reformator-um,* II, 125 (no. 736).

Today the articles of our *Confession* will be presented.

138. (Luther is not quite satisfied with the Confession.)
Luther, *Letter to Melanchthon,* June 29, 1530. Enders,
VIII, 42.

I have received your *Apology,* and wonder at your asking
how far one may yield to the Papists. It is my opinion
that too much has been conceded. I ponder this problem
day and night, looking at it from all sides, searching the
Scriptures, and the longer I contemplate it the more convinced I am of the sure foundation on which our teaching
rests. If God will, not a word shall be withdrawn.

139. The *Confession of Augsburg.* B. J. Kidd, *Documents,*
no. 116. See also *Corpus Reformatorum,* XXVI, 263–
335; and Th. Kolde, *Die älteste Redaktion der Augs-
burger Konfession,* 1906, pp. 4–31.

THE ARTICLES OF FAITH

I. *Of God*

Our churches teach that the decrees of the Council of
Nicea on the unity of the divine essence and on the three
persons are true. They condemn as heretical everything
that has been taught against this article.

II. *Of Original Sin*

Since the fall of Adam all men in their natural state are
born in sin, that is, without fear of God and faith in him,

etc., and that this condition is a real sin which results in the eternal damnation of all those who through baptism and the Holy Spirit have not been born again.

VI. *Of the New Obedience*

This faith (defined in Article V) is bound to produce good works, and it is necessary to perform the good works demanded by God because of God's will, not in order that we may earn with these righteousness before God.

IX. *Of Baptism*

Children ought to be baptized so that they may through baptism be presented to God and be accepted by God's mercy.

X. *Of the Holy Supper*

The body and the blood of Christ are truly present, and are administered to those who partake of the Sacrament.

XI. *Of Confession*

Private absolution is to be retained in the churches, although in the confessional one need not confess all sins. This is in fact impossible.

XII. *Of Penance*

Those who have sinned after baptism may at any time through penance receive forgiveness of sins. Penance consists in two parts. The first is repentance, and the second, faith. From these proceed good works, which are the fruits of penance.

XIII. *Of the Use of the Sacrament*

Sacraments have been instituted not as a sign among men, but as testimonials of God's will toward us, which are to strengthen the faith of those who partake of them.

XIV. *Of Free Will*

Human will has a certain amount of power to render external justice and to distinguish between those things which are subject to reason. But it does not have power without the Holy Spirit to produce the righteousness of God or spiritual righteousness.

SUGGESTED PROBLEMS

1. Make a list of quotations from the works of Luther in which the statements made by him are not to be taken at their face value.

2. Trace the successive changes in Luther's attitude toward the humanists and humanism.

3. Make a special study of the relations between Erasmus and Luther.

4. Describe the influence exerted on Luther by Staupitz and Tauler.

5. Show to how great an extent Luther was at various times motivated by the force of German patriotism.

6. Define Protestantism and determine when Luther ceased to be a real Roman Catholic.

7. Try to discover why Luther experienced such a severe psychological conflict in the monastery, and why his doctrine of justification by faith alone was possibly the logical outcome of his struggle.

8. Compare the theology of Luther with that of Melanchthon, and trace the influence exerted by the one upon the other.

9. Explain Luther's attitude toward princes and peasants in the Peasants' War.

10. Define the term transubstantiation and compare Luther's view on this doctrine with that of Carlstadt, Zwingli, and Calvin.

QUESTIONS

1. Locate Thuringia, Mansfield, Saxony, Eisleben, Eisenach, Magdeburg, Erfurt, and Wittenberg.

2. Was it surprising that Luther's parents believed in the efficacy of corporal punishments?

3. Was Luther's struggle in the monastery to some extent the result of harsh treatment from his parents?

4 Was Erfurt the right kind of a city for a person in search of learning?

5. Who was Aristotle?

6. What is scholasticism, and who are Thomas Aquinas and Occam?

7. Give all the reasons why Luther was induced to enter a monastery.

8. Why should Luther's father have been opposed to his becoming a monk?

9. Why did Luther remain in the monastery after he regretted his first step? Was a person compelled to stay in the monastery before he had finished his novitiate?

10. Why did monks mortify their bodies? Did they do this to an extreme in the Augustinian monasteries?

11. Did mendicant monks have monasteries?

12. Is it true that Luther, when he was on the Lateran Staircase in Rome, received an inspiration regarding justification by faith?

13. Why was Luther disappointed with Rome?

14. How could Luther say that he had learned nothing from the scholastic theologians?

15. Do those people who believe in predestination say that it matters not what one does?

16. Who was Gerson?

17. Did Staupitz understand the nature of Luther's troubles?

18. What is original sin, and how is it supposed to affect man?

19. Did the Church teach that good works could aid in the process of salvation?

20. Did Luther express any Protestant views in his Lectures on the Psalms?

21. Was Luther radical in his criticisms of the Church and the clergy?

22. What is meant by the doctrine of free will?

23. Was Luther's view on the depravity of man the same as that of Gerard Zerbolt?

24. Make a distinction between divine providence and predestination.

25. Define justification, sanctification, and regeneration.

26. What are the *Epistolae Obscurorum Virorum?*

27. Why was Luther displeased with Erasmus even before 1516?

28. Was Luther widely known before the year 1517?

29. What are indulgences, and who was Tetzel?

30. Was Luther in the year 1517 opposed to the whole practice of indulgences?

31. What is the Treasure of Merit of the Church?

32. Why did Luther post his *Ninety-five Theses* on the church door in Wittenberg?

33. How did it happen that those *Theses* immediately caused such widespread comment?

34. Who supported Luther in his attack on the sale of indulgences?

35. Did the Pope intend to give Luther a fair trial?

36. What was Luther's attitude toward scholasticism in 1518?

37. Who was Philip Melanchthon?

38. Was Luther sincere when in March, 1519, he wrote Pope Leo X that he had not the slightest wish to attack the power of the Roman Church or that of the Pope?

39. Is it true that Luther's character was bad?

40. When and why did Luther for the first time express sympathy for the teachings of Hus and the Hussites?

41. What was the subject of the debate between Luther and John Eck in Leipzig?

42. Define the terms Catholic Church, the Church Universal, the Christian Church.

43. When did Luther first question the doctrines of purgatory?

44. What is the papacy, and how did it originate and develop?

45. What does Luther stress more in the years 1520–1530, love or faith?

46. What is meant by the phrase priesthood of all believers?

47. To how great an extent did the Pope exercise temporal power?

48. Which of the three famous treatises written by Luther in 1520 is the most important?

49. Did Luther's view on indulgences undergo any changes between 1518 and 1520?

50. Could Luther's view on the Holy Supper be called consubstantiation?

51. Why did Luther believe in the baptism of little children?

52. Was Luther entirely opposed to monasticism in 1520?

53. Did Luther reject the practice of confirmation?

54. Was Luther opposed to the confession of sins?

55. Why did Luther place the Epistles of the New Testament above the Gospels?

56. Who was Carlstadt, and why did Luther call him a radical?

57. Why did Luther when he married break further away from the Roman Catholic Church?

58. Is it true that some monks turned Protestant in order to get married?

59. Did Luther believe in democracy?

60. How could Luther justify the killing of so many peasants in the Peasants' War?

61. Was Luther's view on predestination and free will still the same in 1525 as it had been in 1516?

62. What did Erasmus have to say about predestination?

63. Was Luther in favor of religious training for young people both in school and church?

64. What is a catechism?

65. Was Luther more opposed to the doctrine of transubstantiation than to that held by Zwingli and other Swiss Protestants?

66. Why did Luther say that Zwingli was not a Christian?

67. Was Luther a more radical reformer than Zwingli and Calvin?

68. Did the Confession of Augsburg represent the teachings of Luther or rather those of Melanchthon?

69. If Luther had written this Confession would it have been so conciliatory?

70. On what doctrines did Luther, Zwingli, and Calvin agree?